THE VICTORIAN KITCHEN
GARDEN COMPANION

HARRY DODSON AND JENNIFER DAVIES

BBC BOOKS

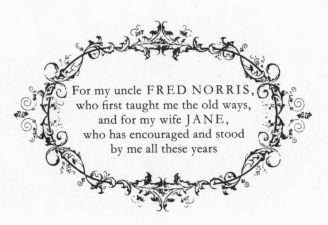

For my uncle FRED NORRIS,
who first taught me the old ways,
and for my wife JANE,
who has encouraged and stood
by me all these years

Published by BBC Books
A division of BBC Enterprises Ltd
Woodlands, 80 Wood Lane, London W12 0TT

First published 1988

ISBN 0 563 20710 8

Typeset in Monophoto Garamond
and printed and bound in England by
Butler and Tanner Ltd, Frome and London
Colour printed by Chorley and Pickersgill, Leeds
Colour separations by Technik, Berkhampsted
Cover printed by Belmont Press, Northampton

CONTENTS

INTRODUCTION

The Victorian age was a time of ingenuity and invention, one-upmanship and interest in science, all rooted in rising affluence and confidence and bound with a strict social hierarchy. Nowhere are these attributes more admirably and amply demonstrated than in the great kitchen gardens of those days. But beautiful and necessary to the great households as these gardens once were, sadly today they are only a nostalgic memory in the minds of people old enough to have experienced the last vestiges of Victorian prosperity in the early decades of this century.

The imposing four-walled gardens themselves (every house of substance had one) have for the most part been lost. Some have disappeared altogether, their foundations sunk beneath modern housing estates and tarmac car parks. Others survive, but are often an embarrassment to their present-day owners. Economy has dictated that behind their locked doors the garden walls enclose nothing but rampant crops of bramble and nettle. Invasive and destructive, the weeds join path to plot and render once tidy plant houses glass-less and crumbling.

Chilton Garden was a perfect example. Located near Hungerford in Berkshire, it had outlived most of its contemporaries and struggled on for a time, competing against cheap imported fruits and deep-frozen vegetables. But eventually, inevitably, it too fell victim to the modern age and its doors were closed.

However, behind the closed doors still lay the bones of a traditional walled kitchen garden. And in Harry Dodson, head gardener at Chilton for over forty years, we had the key to reconstructing and recording for a modern television audience the old skills, plant varieties and horticultural practices before they were lost forever. Harry was a nephew of the head gardener to the Earl of Selborne, and two other uncles were also head gardeners. He had learned his trade from these men, and they in their turn had learned theirs from Victorian predecessors. Harry thus provided a direct link with nineteenth-century husbandry skills and, what's more, had spent over half a century working as a gardener on private estates before retiring (but not severing his connection) from Chilton Garden.

Together, on a cool October morning in 1984, we examined what was left of the walled garden. Chilton had old peach and nectarine houses as well as smaller glasshouses which, in their heyday, would have nurtured melons, cucumbers and tomatoes. In the centre of these, dilapidated but with its Victorian wrought-iron staging still intact, was a large greenhouse – once the 'show' house for impressive and beautiful displays of pot plants, specially placed for inspection by the master of the house on his visits to the kitchen garden. On this first visit the staging was empty, the wrought iron rusty. Box edging around the vegetable plots had outgrown its original diminutive beauty and was now rangy and irregular. A few pear and apple trees still clung to the brickwork, but for the most part, where once fully laden branches of apricots, peaches and nectarines would have spread, the walls were disappointingly bare.

The obstacles were all too obvious, but Harry was enthusiastic to join in the challenge of restoration. Even with his experience and guidance, however, and kind help from several horticultural advisers, the process of turning Chilton back through a century of seasons was inevitably slow. We began by obtaining as many modern seed catalogues as we could find, comparing them with old Victorian seed catalogues. The old ones, their pages thick with lists of forgotten varieties and fine engravings, contrasted oddly with today's thin, glossy versions. Cross-checking between old and new revealed that a few old varieties had still kept their places in the twentieth century, but oddities like the once popular Portuguese cabbage or Couve Tronchuda (brought to Britain in 1821) would be hard to find.

Soft fruits for the garden plots and fruit trees for the walls also had to be found. We again checked old lists against new, but here we had an additional handicap – not only did we want nineteenth-century varieties but we needed them partly trained, either as fan shapes for the peach, nectarine, plum and cherry trees, or as espaliers or cordons for the apples and pears. That is how they would have been grown, as beautiful to the eye as they were productive. We found that the demise of the old estate kitchen gardens over the years had brought a corresponding decline in nurseries which still trained fruit trees. The combination of time and knowledge that such trees need is something which most of today's gardeners don't have, and modern nurseries find it just isn't worth the trouble to produce trained trees. Consequently we failed in some respects. For instance, it proved impossible to find the old, green Cornish Gillyflower apple trained as an espalier – indeed it was difficult enough to find it listed at all. However, by contacting a wide number of nurseries, we eventually accumulated sufficient and various old varieties to plant against the 12-foot-high brick walls. For the warm south-facing wall we had nectarines, peaches, apricots, early sweet cherries and the choicest dessert plums. For the east- and west-facing walls we had dessert apples and pears and, for the cool north-facing wall at the bottom of the garden, pears, culinary plums and dark red Morello cherries.

Posts and rails were set in to flank some of the vegetable plots and against these, as they might have been years ago, old culinary varieties of apples such as Lord Derby and Warner's King were trained. Box edging and the basic culinary herbs a Victorian cook would have demanded from the garden were planted.

It took two years of planning, repairing, planting and tending before the garden was ready for the BBC television cameras and a small team led by producer Keith Sheather. Only then, with the help of Peter Thoday, a horticultural historian and himself the son of a head gardener, did our year of recording a Victorian kitchen garden, season by season, actually begin.

Peter, with his knowedge of botany and science, commented on the values of the old varieties and the efficiency of such simple structures as hotbeds, which forwarded a crop by several weeks. He also measured the temperature of the walls and came up with the surprising information that, built as they were on a south-facing slope, these old kitchen gardens could be as warm as the south of France near the south-facing wall, while at the same time, the ground beneath the north-facing wall at the bottom of the garden could be as cool as north Yorkshire!

The garden under Harry's care became a beautiful place, with perfectly trained fruit trees and vegetable crops planted with an eye to texture and colour as well as productiveness. Neat box edging divided path from plot and, where a plot met a pathway, a footscraper ensured that soil from garden boots did not sully the raked gravel. Flowers bloomed from early spring to late summer in six-foot broad borders either side of the central pathway; cordon-trained pears and apples met across iron arches, forming first a canopy of blossom and then, as autumn came, fruit above the heads of visitors walking beneath.

I

2

3

4

5

6

7

9

10

Throughout the year Harry demonstrated the old arts and crafts of gardening that he had learned from boyhood onwards, including the skills needed to make the garden provide luxuries: pineapples, melons and strawberries at Christmas, and salad the year round. At the same time, the garden had to provide sufficient variety and quantity of ordinary produce to feed a host of servants every day of the year. Harry showed how planting trees against different walls increased the span of their cropping season; that lantern handlights could bring on early salading in the south-facing border; and that lettuces could be cut cool and crisp from the north border even on the hottest summer day. He explained how, in the iron-hard days of winter, terracotta forcing pots could help to provide pale succulent branches of seakale and stalks of rhubarb, how the old peach houses could give shelter to early peas and potatoes grown in pots, and carrots the 'size of a lady's finger' could be raised on hotbeds as winter delicacies. Harry used fertilisers which had never seen the inside of a packet, demonstrated old ways of dealing with pests, showed the merits of successional sowing, 'catch-crops', pruning, training and a host of other skills needed to keep the kitchen garden a beautiful and productive paradise.

This small volume has been compiled as a 'companion' to *The Victorian Kitchen Garden*, the book I wrote to record the re-making of the garden and the re-discovery of the old plant varieties its walls once contained. It is also a tribute to the garden itself, and to all those who helped in its restoration. It is *not* a book to be followed, word for word, for practical instruction, though I hope that Harry's comments, tips and stories will prove useful and inspirational for many gardeners. It is (I hope) an entertaining reminder of a year in the cloistered yet productive world of the nineteenth-century kitchen garden. As *The Cottage Gardener and Country Gentleman's Companion* commented in 1856, 'Some people may say "This reading and writing so much, what good is it?" ... In gardening matters it is this good – you can refer to the past, and see how it corresponds with the present, and, from the experience thus gained, the course for the future can be the more easily shaped out.'

Jennifer Davies

PHOTOGRAPHS ON PREVIOUS PAGES
1 The restored garden at Chilton through an archway in the east wall.
2 A pyramid-shaped potato clamp made in late summer.
3 The warm south-facing wall and border.
4 Hurdles and handlights cosset and protect vegetable crops.
5 Harry cuts flowers to dress the dining-room table.
6 Blossom on an Early Rivers peach, a Victorian variety.
7 Frontispiece of a 19th-century gardeners' instruction manual.
8 The peach and fig houses at Chilton.
9 Melons ripen, supported by nets.
10 Victorian engraving of Little Heath and Queen Anne's Pocket melons.
11 Apples spread against the west-facing wall at Chilton.
12 The Show House where flowering plants were specially staged to please 'The Family'.

JANUARY

In the garden January is the last month for preparation for spring and summer, for the process of vegetation will soon be in full progress.
Beeton's Shilling Gardening, 1874

—◆—

Radishes – In the beginning, or at any time this month, when the weather is open, sow some short-topped radishes for an early crop, on a warm border, that lies well to the sun, under a wall or other fence; and about the middle or latter end of the month you may sow more of the same sort, and some salmon radishes to succeed the short top.

Harry A better way than sowing on a warm border is to get your early radishes by intercropping them with lettuce in a frame. Plant the lettuce 8 to 9 inches apart in rows 10 inches apart and sow a row of radish between the rows of lettuce. The radish will be cleared before the lettuce is ready for cutting.

Carrots – Sow a few Early Horn on a south border. Examine those stored up, and remove any that are proving unsound; take off young growths, if any are being made.

Harry Sowing carrots on an early border can be carried out from the end of January onwards, provided you can walk on the soil without it sticking to your boots. If the weather turns bad afterwards, it doesn't matter as a rule, because the seed will lay in the ground until the weather improves.

THERE is a difference of several weeks in the climate of different parts of the country; operations that should be performed at once in the South, may thus be generally deferred for several weeks in the North.

The seasonal directions being calculated for the meridian of London, it may be useful to the reader, if we quote the comparative heat of the sun at several degrees of latitude, from the Rev. John Lawrence's *Pleasures and Profits of Gardening*, 1000 being the unit, of which the following are parts:

Places	Latitude	Heat June 10	Heat Apr 10 & Aug 12	Heat Mar 10 & Sept 12
Lyons	46	880	711	516
Paris	49	814	631	431
The Lizard	50	800	614	413
London	$51\frac{1}{2}$	777	597	388
Bedford	52	770	579	379
Northampton	$52\frac{1}{2}$	767	574	375
Boston	53	757	561	362
Lincoln	$53\frac{1}{2}$	753	555	357
York	54	742	543	346
Newcastle	55	726	524	320
Edinburgh	56	711	506	312

Mint – Make a small hot-bed for some mint, when it is required at
an early season in young green shoots for salads and mint sauce, &c.

Harry The pot method is easier. Mint in a pot placed in a cold frame or
unheated glasshouse will advance by a month on that outside. The earliest
mint will stand a little heat and will thus provide shoots of picking length
by late January, early February. I knew some places where mint was a
permanent feature in peach houses, also clumps of rhubarb. You put the
rhubarb in a corner where it didn't interfere with anything or anybody.
Timperley Early is a good variety of rhubarb for a cool house.

Parsley – Protect a portion from severe frost. Sow a little in a
sheltered situation.

Harry If you sow pots of parsley in August and September and keep them
under cover, you can have parsley all winter. If supplies are expected each
week, a cold frame sown up in these months will give quite good supplies
throughout all but the hardest of winters. If heated houses are available,
seed sown in 60°F in January will give usable parsley by mid March.

Tomatoes – If some of these are required early, sow in heat, for
transplanting under glass, in February and March.

Harry If glass and heat are available, early tomatoes can even be sown in
November and December. Grow as near the glass as possible in a temperature of 60°F and pot on as required in pots 9 or 10 inches wide. Allow
three to five trusses, then remove the tops – the first pick would be in April.

Fruit trees

Where there are wall and espalier apple and pear trees yet unpruned,
that work should be forwarded as much as possible, and may be safely
performed upon all sorts, without fearing any danger from frost
injuring the trees in the cut parts, even if it happens when performing
the operation.
Peaches, nectarines, and apricots may be pruned and nailed any time
in this month if the weather should prove mild; or at all opportunities,
without danger of any material injury, if pruned in frosty weather.

Harry This is good advice. Seize upon every spell of fine weather so all
the pruning is done by early March. Otherwise you'll start knocking
buds off, and by March you'll be wanting to get on with other jobs.

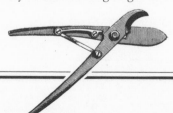

Cauliflowers – Look over, in open weather, the frames of cauliflower
plants which were raised and planted in frames last autumn for
protection in winter; to plant out in spring for the principal summer
crops; and where withered or damaged leaves appear, let them be
picked off, and suffer no weeds to grow among them, and stir the
surface gently between, which will enliven and cherish the plants.

Harry According to this, cauliflowers were planted in frames. That's
something I've never done. Cauliflowers are an important crop, always
have been. I sow them in a tray in October and put the tray in a greenhouse.
About 14 days after sowing, that's sometime in November, I prick them
off into 3 or $3\frac{1}{2}$-inch pots. I put the pots in a cold frame or cold greenhouse
and if the weather's severe I cover the frame over, but the greenhouse
normally comes through.

Throughout winter on favourable occasions it's important to keep them
watered. Cauliflower seedlings and young plants should never be allowed
to become dry because that affects the curd.

The forwardest of the plants should be planted out into cold frames or
into large pots and put into a cool peach house towards the end of February.
They should be producing small heads by the end of April.

During the early part of March you can attempt to harden off the
remainder (still in pots). Take the lights off or leave the greenhouse open
or stand the pots out under a south wall. Then plant them on an early
border or intercrop with early peas. With good management, with one
sowing in October you can get cauliflowers by the second week in April
and then right through to July by planting in different places.

Planting Raspberries – You may now make fresh plantations of
raspberries, observing to procure young plants that are furnished
each with one strong shoot of last summer ... preferring those with
good fibrous roots, rejecting such whose roots are naked and woody;
prune off the weak tops of the shoots, and the long straggling roots,
and plant them, by opening small apertures with a spade, in rows four
feet and a half asunder, and two or three feet distance in each row.

Harry Newly planted raspberries must be cut down to within 6 to 9 inches
of ground level – they cannot carry a crop and make new canes for next
year in the first year of planting.

NOTES

NOW is the proper time about the latter end
of this month to begin to make a hot-bed to
raise a few early strawberries; those which are
planted now in a hot-bed will produce fruit fit
to gather in March or April.

Everyman His Own Gardener, 1845

Currants and *gooseberries* may also be planted; and if the trees are to be placed round the quarters of the kitchen garden, or in cross rows to divide the ground into wide compartments, you should prune them up to one clean stem of about ten, twelve, or fifteen inches, before you form the head of the tree; for when these trees are suffered to branch away immediately from the bottom, they, by spreading out so near the ground, will impede the growth of any crops that grow near their low expansion, and render it troublesome to work about them, in the occasional business of digging, hoeing, weeding, &c.; besides they do not appear so agreeable as when trained to a single stem supporting a regular head of branches.

Harry You could leave gooseberry pruning until the end of February. It used to be the practice to leave it all winter in some establishments, because last year's growth would protect the buds from birds during the winter.

Potatoes – Plant some of the Ash-leaved Kidney, or any good early sort, in small pots, one set in each. The pots may then be piled together in any warm place, either light or dark, till the potato shoots are about to appear, when the plants should be turned out and planted on a slight hot-bed, 18 inches by 8 inches apart. Some may also be grown to maturity in pots.

Harry I've got early potatoes by potting them up in January in 10-inch pots and putting them under the vines in a vinery or in an early peach house. A temperature of 55°F at an early stage gives them a good start, and as the weather gets better the temperature rises as well. At the same time, it's a good idea to pot up Dwarf French beans, 5 to 6 beans to a pot. Fill only half the pot with old potting soil, and when you've placed the beans in the pot cover them with about an inch of the soil. Top dress with the old potting soil when the beans clear the top of the pot. Like the potatoes, they need a minimum of 55°F to get them started. When the beans get to a height of 9 inches, support them with two or three bushy sticks, 12 to 15 inches high, either bits of old besom broom or the tops of pea sticks. The potato haulm (stalk) is also best if afforded some brushwood or four canes, 18 inches high, for support. In each case, a tie of bast or green twist should be run around each ring of support about half the height of the sticks.

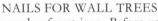

NAILS FOR WALL TREES

These should be made of cast-iron. Before using them, make them red-hot, and then throw them into cold linseed oil. This gives them a varnish which preserves them from rusting, and prevents the mortar of the wall sticking to them when they are drawn.

The Gardener's Receipt Book, 1861

A CURE
for Burns & Scalds

Bruise an onion and a potato in a mortar; add a tablespoon of salad-oil, and apply this pulp to the naked burn or scald; secure it with a bandage.

Housekeeper's & Butler's Assistant, 1862

FEBRUARY

*The mean temperature of February is
nearly two degrees higher than January, and the average number of frosty nights is
about eleven. Less rain falls this month than in any other, and hoar-frosts at this
time generally precede it.*
Beeton's Shilling Gardening, 1874

Continue to manure, dig, or trench all vacant ground when the
weather will permit, performing these operations, however, only in
dry weather. Protect, if necessary, with litter, spruce branches, &c.,
such things as require protection.

Liquorice – If the weather permit, plant cuttings of the
roots. *Horse radish* – plant in ground well trenched and
manured. *Garlic* – Plant in drills. Set the cloves two or three
inches deep, and from six to nine inches apart. *Dill* – May be
sown in the end of the month. *Fennel* – Sow in shallow drills.

Harry This is the perennial fennel, not the bulbous Florence fennel. Sowing
the bulbous fennel takes place in late April, followed by successive sowings
until early July.

Jerusalem Artichokes – Plant in any spare part of the garden.

Harry I'd put them in a corner of the garden. They're not an elegant plant
and can take sun off crops. You can leave them in the ground during the
winter and late February/early March clear off the haulm and give them a
dressing of potting soil or short manure.

Dig an open quarter of ground the beginning of this month for a full
crop of *beans*. Windsor, Token, Sandwich, and other large beans, are
proper to plant at this season for the main crop.

Harry Broad beans can lay in the ground for a long time without coming
to harm, so you *can* sow in February.

You may now venture on sowings of many things with a chance of
success, in proper situations – Early Horn carrots, scarlet short-top
radishes, Bath Cos lettuces, celery, parsnips . . . Do not be disheartened
if they fail, but at them again. A stout-hearted gardener will never
say die.

Harry With parsnips, it always used to be the principle to sow as soon as
you could get the seeds in, because they used to think you wouldn't get a
good crop if you waited. But now it's been proved that you can sow as late
as April and still get a good crop.

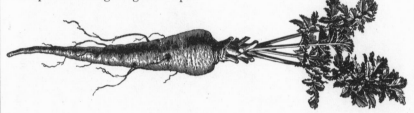

Shallots – Plant the bulbs in newly trenched ground at the distance
of six inches from each other, in shallow drills one foot apart.

Harry You need a good piece of ground for shallots, similar but not quite
so good as for onions. For ease of working, plant the shallots a foot each
way, that's a foot in the row and the rows a foot apart. They are a dirty
little crop because, of course, there's no foliage to stifle weeds, and if you
only plant them 6 inches apart you'll knock the 'pipes' about when you're
hoeing and weeding. If you don't wish to bother with spring onions for
early pulling, plant the shallots 6 inches apart in the rows. You can pull
every other one out and use it as a spring onion, still leaving the main crop
standing at 12 inches apart.

Fruit trees of all sorts may be planted any time this month, when the
weather is open. Let every kind be planted at proper distances, both
for walls, espaliers, and in standards, that they may have room to
grow without interfering with each other in the space of a few years;
which is often the case in many gardens, more particularly wall trees.

Harry Planting can continue up until the middle of March, but the earlier
you plant the better. The ideal time to start is the middle of February. If,
however, you have fruit trees of your own propagation, the finest time to
transplant is October, just before the leaves begin to show signs of having
finished their useful life. Water well and shade from the sun if it's bright –
they will make root again well before the fall and really get away with a
good start in the coming year. This was a usual practice in lots of large
private gardens before the War.

_____
_____
_____
_____
_____
_____
_____
_____
_____
_____
_____
_____
_____

KEEP the gravel walks perfectly free from weeds, moss and litter of any sort; and let them be well rolled occasionally in dry weather.

To Render Leather Waterproof

North American Recipe: Boil together for half an hour one quart of linseed oil, two ounces of resin, and half an ounce of powdered white vitriol; remove the mixture from the fire, and add four ounces of spirit of turpentine, and two ounces of very fine and very dry oak sawdust, mix well and apply with a brush.

The Cottage Gardener, 1850

In February, March and April every greenhouse or conservatory may be rendered beautiful to look at and delightful in fragrance by a few climbing roses. Roses are valued at all times according to their abundance and time of blooming, but if there is one time more than another at which they are justly esteemed it is in the early spring months.

The Journal of Horticulture, 1877

Rhubarb – Make fresh plantations by dividing the roots in pieces, with a bud to each. Plant these three feet from each other, in rows four feet apart. ❧ *Mustard* – Make successional sowings in a warm situation every week, or as often as required.

Harry As early in the year as this, it would be safer to sow mustard in a cold frame at least – but, better still, in a standard seed box sown each week in a warm greenhouse.

Clean the stems of *fruit trees* from moss and scale, if any such exist, choosing a moist time for the operation. Use, in the first place, for the moss, a piece of hard-wood with triangular edges; then, with a hard scrubbing brush, sand and water, scour off all extraneous matters from the stem. Look out, in pruning, for the eggs of insects glued in rings on the young shoots; remove and effectually destroy them. Syringe peach trees after nailing, and before the blossom buds are too far advanced, with sulphur and water thoroughly mixed; with this, also, the whole surface of the wall should be well syringed.

Harry When I was a lad working at the rectory at Blackmoor in Hampshire, the parson made me paint his fruit trees with a mixture of soft soap and paraffin. In the 1920s, tar oil washes began to be used and proved a good way of burning off insect eggs and cleaning up fruit trees. I use a tar oil wash on the trees at Chilton.

Laying Turf

Grass turf may be laid any time this month, where wanted, either to make new or mend old work, for it will now grow freely with little trouble; observing to beat it well, and roll it with a heavy roller now and then, to make the surface firm and even.

Planting Hedges

Plant hedges where wanted, especially deciduous kinds, such as hawthorn, privet, white-thorn, hornbeam, beech, elder, elm, &c. Likewise is a proper time to plash old hedges, that are run up naked, or open below.

Box for edging to border, &c. may be planted any time in this month; it will take root in a short time, and there will be no fear of its success; likewise, where there are gaps in any former planted edgings let the deficiencies be made good; also old overgrown or irregular edgings replanted; for nothing looks worse than ragged and irregular box edgings by the sides of the walks.

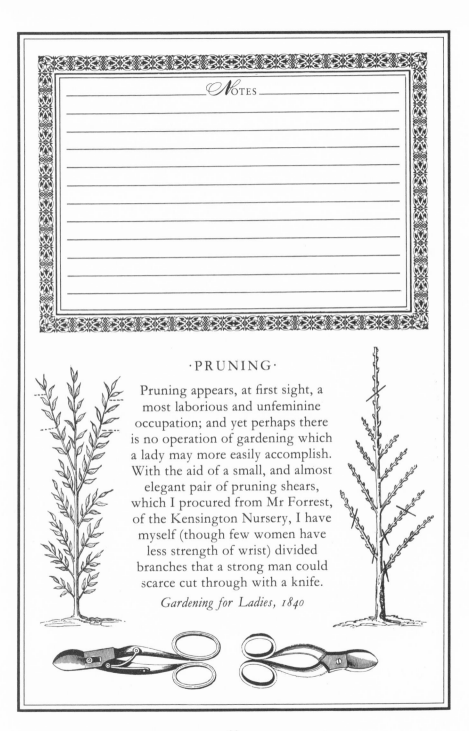

·PRUNING·

Pruning appears, at first sight, a
most laborious and unfeminine
occupation; and yet perhaps there
is no operation of gardening which
a lady may more easily accomplish.
With the aid of a small, and almost
elegant pair of pruning shears,
which I procured from Mr Forrest,
of the Kensington Nursery, I have
myself (though few women have
less strength of wrist) divided
branches that a strong man could
scarce cut through with a knife.

Gardening for Ladies, 1840

Sow a principal crop of *peas* the beginning of this month in an open piece of ground; you may still continue sowing a succession of the hotspurs, and other small kinds, and it is now a fine season to sow full crops of the large peas, such as marrowfats, rouncivals, &c.

Harry I'd sow 12 or 15 peas in pots in early February. The peas would be 2 or 3 inches by the end of February or early March. Then I'd harden them off ready for planting out, 10 to 12 inches apart in the rows, 3 to 4 feet between the rows depending on the height of the variety. It's best to put pea sticks with them immediately, with plenty of brushwood at the bottom of the sticks to give protection.

Cauliflower, lettuce, radish, early cabbage and round-headed spinach can all be sown and planted down the middle of the rows, gaining protection from the peas as they grow and making full use of the ground. This was a regular practice in days gone by at Chilton, when the peas were planted and stuck and intercropped with cabbage, cauliflowers, lettuce, beet and spinach. It was a lovely sight, and the finish of the work was really first class.

Leeks – Sow some in the last week.

Harry Sow leeks preferably in a cold frame, making the main sowing in the open in late March/early April.

Cabbage (Red) – Sow some in the end of the month.

Harry A March/early April sowing of red cabbage will give you the main crop, which is used for the pickle cabbage for winter storing.

Preparing for Grafting
Grafting may be begun any time after the fifteenth or twentieth of this month, provided the weather be mild.
The sorts proper to begin with, are *pears*, *plums*, and *cherries*; and these kinds generally succeed remarkably well, when grafted sometime in the last fortnight of this month.

GRAFTING WAX

Take common sealing-wax, any colour but green, one part, mutton fat one part, white soap one part, honey one-eighth part. Melt the wax and the fat first, then add the white soap, gradually stirring the while; and lastly put in the honey, just before taking the whole off the fire. It should be poured hot into paper moulds, and kept slightly stirred till it begins to harden.

The Gardener's Receipt Book, 1861

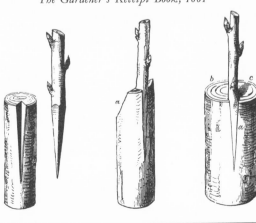

MARCH

*ain Crops and March both begin with
an M. Remember that they are even more closely connected than that. Plant and sow
all sorts of things.*
The Kitchen Garden, 1859

When *apricot*, *peach*, and *nectarine* trees are in blossom, some of the
choice kinds should be defended from frost, if it should happen at
that time, by covering the trees with mats, &c. The mats for this
purpose should be of the large size; one end of them should be
fastened with nails or hooks to the top of the wall, and let them hang
down over the trees. The lower end of the mat should also be
fastened down, to prevent their being blown to and fro by the wind,
which would beat the blossoms off.
When the weather is mild, the mats should be taken off: for it is only
in sharp frosts and cutting frosty winds that the blossom requires to
be thus sheltered.

It is scarcely necessary to observe the weeds should be destroyed
wherever they are seen to exist . . .

Harry The time to hoe is when there aren't any weeds!

Salsify – A little may be sown in drills 8 to 10 inches asunder, but
not the main crop.

Harry Salsify's a winter crop. In all my training I've never sown it as early
as March. To me there's no point in sowing so early, as this would make
it ready for pulling in August when you won't really need it. There's an
abundance of other vegetables available then.

CRESS

It is ungrateful to say a word against cresses, but it may be as well to remember that in England at least they have come to mean curses. 'I don't care a curse' really means, 'I don't care a cress.' Perhaps we have too much of them. They are (putting asparagus out of account, which has a short season and a dear price) the one vegetable eaten by rich and poor in England, for health even more than for food.

Kettner's Book of the Table, 1877

Iron is cheap; therefore, don't be afraid of wearing out your hoe and rake.

Nasturtiums are often used in families; their flowers and young leaves for salads, the flowers also to garnish dishes, and their green berries to pickle.

    This is now a good time to sow them: and the sooner in the month, the better.

Everyman His Own Gardener, 1845

Broccoli − Sow Walcheren, and other sorts towards the end of the month.
Some should be sown in a cold frame, more especially if, owing to
frost or wet, the soil elsewhere is in bad condition for the
seeds. *Brussels Sprouts* − Sow a little in the first week to come
in early; and towards the end of the month for the main crop.
Cabbages − Sow, about the middle of the month, the Early York,
Early Battersea, Vanack, or Fulham, for summer and autumn supply.

Harry All the brassica family can be sown in March. It's not ready as a rule
for planting out until June.

Savoys − Savoy-seed for a principal crop, to serve the family from
about Michaelmas to Christmas, should be sown about the middle
or towards the latter end of the month in an open situation. But if it
is desired to have Savoys well cabbaged earlier in autumn, that is,
in the end of August, or any time in September, they should be sown
in February, or at least the first week of this month. The sorts of
Savoys are the green, yellow, and white; but the green kind is to be
preferred for the main crop.

Harry It's best to sow Savoys in a seedbed, with drills a foot apart. Use a
little hoe to make a flat drill, which will give you more space for the seeds.
Plant out the young plants in June.

Beet – A little may be sown for autumn use, also some of the White
or Silver Leaf-beet.

Harry Sowing beetroot in the old days was a dodgy business. They didn't
have varieties which wouldn't bolt, and often just when it looked as though
the beetroot would bulb up, it would go to seed. Today we've got varieties
which are bred to be bolt hardy. A March sowing in a cold frame will give
young, delicious, small beet in May.

Peas – Sow *marrowfat peas* once a fortnight or three weeks at farthest;
by which means you will have a constant supply of young peas for
the table ... All the sorts of peas should now be sown in open
situations, not much under low spreading trees.

Harry Sow peas very late in March. It's best to leave the tall marrowfat
kinds until early April.

American cress may be sown.

Harry American cress is a good substitute for watercress, but watch it
because it can become a weed. It seeds itself and creeps all over the place.
Its yellow flowers are quite attractive in a border or odd corner. It's an
accommodating plant and will grow freely anywhere.

Asparagus – Sow in drills 18 inches apart. Make new plantations.
Dress beds.

_____

'Time and tide will wait for no man', and the short season of growth, that we are permitted to take advantage of, is passing away, while langour and insipidity and inertness may be characterising our actions.

The preparation of the ground and the sowing of seeds form two of the chief duties of the month. March is generally looked upon as an inauspicious month for out-door operations in connexion with seed-sowing, but in this ever-variable climate of ours, we must lose no time.
The Villa Gardener, March 1871

Protect wall-trees by nets, thin canvas, straw screens, spruce branches, fern, or by other means that may be at command.
The Gardener's Assistant, 1859

APRIL

Put not your faith in a mild winter – April is sometimes more cruel than January.
The Gardener's Record, 1870

Small Birds – To scare from Seeds
There are many ways of effecting this, by nets, etc., but a simple
mode of doing it is to stick a few potatoes all over with white feathers,
and suspend them a few inches from the ground, by means of a few
threads of red worsted passed across your seedbeds.

Harry The old cottagers on Blackmoor Estate frequently used to do this
to scare the birds – didn't do a great deal of good, but it made them happy!
It's interesting that red thread is recommended. In days gone by, one of
the old men I used to work with reckoned that pigeons were allergic to the
colour red. He made us paint bottles red and hang them up. But it was
probably my old 'bangers' which did the trick. The bangers were special
cartridges threaded on to a fuse line which I'd hang between two sheets of
corrugated iron. I wasn't very popular in the neighbourhood!

Lavender – Sow or propagate by cuttings and
slips. *Nasturtiums* – Sow nasturtium-seed; draw a drill or drills,
about an inch deep, and a yard asunder, or a single drill under a fence,
&c., on which to train the plants in their running growth; sow the
seed moderately thin, and cover it in regularly with the earth.
Onions and *leeks* may yet be sown the beginning of the month, for
they will not succeed well if sown later, but especially the onions,
which will not bulb effectually; or you may now sow onions on a
light, poorish soil, to produce small bulbs for pickling. *Parsnips* –
Sow early in the month.
Thyme – Sow in light soil, or propagate by dividing the
plant. *Parsley* – Hamburgh parsley, which is cultivated for its
roots, should be sown in the beginning of the month. The French
Large-rooted variety is the best. The Dwarf Curled, which is the
best variety for garnishing, may also be sown.

Harry Most herbs can be sown in situ this month.

Notes

Aspect & Character of the Month

The temperature is lowest at sunrise, and there are, on average of ten years, six frosty nights in the month. An unusual fall of rain in April is supposed to indicate a dry season for the harvest.

Beeton's Shilling Gardening, 1874

Weeds will now begin to appear plentifully from seed in every part of the garden. The utmost diligence should be used to destroy them while they are young, before they get the start of the crops; especially towards the middle and latter end of this month, when, if a forward season, they will be advancing in rapid growth.

Beet – Sow the main crop, from the middle to the end of the month. In dry weather the seed should be steeped a day before sowing.

Harry A better and safer remedy in any dry weather with all seed sowing is to water the drills well before sowing. Some flower seeds can be soaked but, as a rule, only beans and peas in the vegetable kingdom.

Beans – Sow successions; draw earth up to those already up. *Borage* – Sow a little for a succession. *Caraway* – Sow if not done in autumn. Thin the plants to 8 inches apart. *Cardoons* – Sow, about the middle of the month, in patches of three seeds, 18 inches from patch to patch, in well-manured trenches 4 feet apart.

Harry With cardoons, seeds sown in pots is safer. Then plant out in May.

❖≻❈❈❈❈≺❖

Carrots – Sow in succession.

Harry Sow successions of carrots up until the first week of July.

❖≻❈❈❈❈≺❖

Celeriac – Sow thinly in rows 12 inches apart, for plants to blanch in winter. *Endive* – Sow a small quantity of the fine curled Italian, to come in early. *Fennel* – Sow, or plant slips, if not done last month. *Kohlrabi* – A little of the Early White Vienna may be sown at the end of the month, for use when young, instead of turnips, if these should fail in very hot dry weather.

Harry Kohlrabi is best eaten when it's small. I always picked it for the dining room when it was not much bigger than a walnut.

❖≻❈❈❈❈≺❖

Potatoes may yet be successfully planted, if it was omitted in the last month; but they should be planted the first or second week in this month, that they may attain good perfection for use forward in autumn, and full growth by October.

Harry Potatoes may be planted as late as the first week in June and still give a good crop – not quite so good, of course, if the season is very dry.

Flowers in a Garden – To Arrange
The Cavendish Society recommend blue flowers to be placed next to
orange, and violet next to the yellow; whilst red and pink flowers are never
to be seen to greater advantage than when surrounded by verdure and by
white flowers: the latter may also be advantageously dispersed among
groups of blue and orange, and violet and yellow flowers. Plants whose
flowers are to produce a contrast should be of the same size; and in many
cases the colour of the sand or gravel-walks, or beds of a garden, should
be made to conduce to the general effect.

The Gardener's Receipt Book, 1861

Ink for Zinc Labels – Take 1 drachm
of verdigris, 1 drachm of sal-ammoniac
powder and half-a-drachm of lamp-black,
and mix them with 10 drachms of water;
and this will form an indelible ink for
writing on zinc.

Sow *peas* to succeed those sown in March. Where a constant supply of peas are required, there should be some sown at least every fortnight or three weeks ... Draw earth to such rows of peas which are come up and advanced a little height. This will strengthen the plants, and forward them greatly in their growth.

Harry When you sow peas (and broad beans), a good labour-saving tip is to sow them in a single drill. This means that you can hoe right up close to the plants, thus doing away with much of the hand weeding.

Purslane – May now be sown, if warm dry weather, on a bed of light rich earth, in the common ground. Sow it either in drill six inches asunder, or evenly on the surface, and rake it in lightly and regularly. Water the bed often in dry weather, and shade it from the hot sun till the plants are come up, and have gotten a little strength ... This plant being of a moist cold nature, is by many people much esteemed to use in summer salads.

Salsify – Sow, in the end of the month, in rows one foot apart. *Scorzonera* – Sow the principal crop in the end of the month. *Sea Kale* – In the beginning of the month sow seeds, or propagate by cuttings of the roots, if new plantations are required. *Shallots* – Hoe and loosen the soil about the plants. *Skirret* – Sow on rich, light soil, and afterwards thin to six inches apart.

》》ﷺﷺﷺﷺﷺ《《

Fruit Trees – Disbud when any of the shoots have pushed so far as to require removal; but let this be done sparingly at first, and always gradually. If cold weather check, in a great measure, the flow of the sap, desist from checking it still more by disbudding, till the circulation again becomes more active.

》》ﷺﷺﷺﷺﷺ《《

Thin *apricots*, where they are produced too thick on the trees; especially where they are in clusters, and the young fruit a little advanced in growth nearly as big as the largest peas or the end of a little finger, which they sometimes are, in forward springs, by the latter end of this month, which will be time enough to begin that work. Observe in thinning them, to leave the most promising and best shaped fruit; but do not leave the fruit so close together as, in their advancing growth, to thrust one another off the branches. The young green fruit thinned off as above may generally be saved for tarts, for which they are excellent; and will now be highly acceptable for that occasion.

REGISTERED HAND GARDEN SEED DRILL.—
Four thousand sent out in 1868 and 1869. At the
Great German International Agricultural Exhibi-
tion, Altona, Hamburgh (1869), the First-class Silver
Medal was awarded to JOSIAH LE BUTT for
his Manufactures; also at the Great German International Horticultural Exhibition, Hamburgh, 1869,
another First-class Silver Medal was awarded. By
simply turning a screw, this Drill can at once be
adapted for Sowing Onions,
Cabbage, Cauliflowers, Broccoli,
Barley, Wheat, Sainfoin, Mangel
Wurzel, Tares, Rape, Turnips,
Flax, and Carrot Seeds. It is an
invaluable implement for a
Market Gardener, and to all who
possess a Kitchen Garden; and for
the Farm it will be found useful for the purpose of filling up the places
where the horse-drill has missed. It can easily be worked by a lad.

Full directions sent with each Drill. On receipt of stamps or Post-
office Order, made payable to JOSIAH LE BUTT, Patentee and
Manufacturer of the Champion Haymaker, Bury St Edmund's, a Drill
will be sent immediately. Price 12s. 6d. The name of the nearest station
should be given.

MAY

*As the warm weather progresses, the
gardener should be on the alert, in order to conquer the various kinds of insects.
The Kitchen Gardener's Instructor, 1860*

—————●◆●—————

Celery – Prepare trenches for an early crop, $3\frac{1}{2}$ or 4 feet apart, 1 spit
deep and 18 inches wide, laying the earth with a good slope, in order
to catch the rain. Abundance of manure, consisting of a mixture of
cow-dung and rotten stable-dung, should be dug in the bottom of
the trenches. Carefully remove all suckers from the plants; then plant
them about 9 inches apart, and water immediately.

Egg Plants – Towards the end of the month some of these may be
planted out in a rich, warm border, at the foot of a south wall.

Harry Eggplants need to be very well protected. It's safer to plant them
in a frame.

Engine for Watering the Branches of Trees

For the purpose of watering the branches of infested wall-trees, in dry hot weather, there is nothing so convenient as a hand-watering engine, generally made of tin, or sometimes of copper, of small or larger dimensions, worked by means of a small single-handed pump, fixed therein, to discharge the water in a stream from a pipe to turn in any direction.

By the help of this small engine, a person may stand on the walks, and with great ease and expedition throw the water in a strong stream against any part of the wall-trees, from the bottom to the top of the wall, and is the readiest, most expeditious, and effectual method of watering the branches of these trees, for the engine will throw the water with such considerable  force against the trees as to displace caterpillars, and other insects, and will effectually clear the leaves and branches from dust, cobwebs, and from any sort of filth they may have contracted; and if the waterings are often repeated, in dry weather, where insects at any time appear, it will greatly diminish their increase, and prevent their spreading considerably. This engine may also be used occasionally in watering the branches of espalier-trees, and young or old standard trees, where attacked by insects; also occasionally in watering different parts of the garden in a dry season.

Examine all seed-beds, in order to detect failures, and if there are any, sow again immediately. The hoe should now be employed among rising crops.

Water only when absolutely necessary; but when watering is performed, it should be done effectually.

Cabbages – Plant out for principal summer crops as soon as the plants in the seed-beds are fit, taking advantage of cloudy weather, if such occur. It is better to plant when the weather is likely to change from dry to wet, than in the end of a wet period.

Leeks – Sow for a late crop, and transplant the earlier sown ones.

Harry The leeks sown now, particularly the good old Musselburgh variety, will stay in the ground until wanted right through the coming winter and following early spring.

Onions – Sow in the beginning of the month, for pickling. Hoe, thin, and weed.

Harry No need to hoe. Leave as sown, and one will choke the other out.

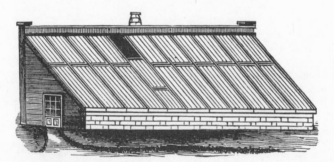

The Fig House – Maintain generally a moist atmosphere; syringe frequently, except when the fruit is ripening. Water with manure water occasionally, but not if the plants are growing too vigorously. Take care that the plants do not suffer one hour for want of water.

Harry The figs should have all shoots except the extension shoots stopped at five leaves, and sub laterals stopped at two leaves.

Peach and Nectarine Houses – Examine the borders, so that, if necessary, they may be rendered sufficiently moist before the fruit begins to colour; for if not done before that takes place, it cannot afterwards, without affecting the flavour of the fruit.

Harry It makes the fruit watery if you water too much when it's colouring up. Airing should be freely given when the ripening begins.

CARROT

Those that would grow this useful root
Free from blight and maggots,
Must freely use both lime and soot,
And they will have fine carrots.

William Gain, Gardener, Lynewood, 1877

Ants – to Expel

Ants may be expelled by shaking flowers of sulphur over
the nest, or place, where they resort. This will not kill them,
but will drive them from the spot. Ants have also a very
great dislike to passing over chalk, and may be effectually
prevented from passing up the stems of trees, by making a
circle round the stem with chalk, an inch and a half or two
inches broad.

The Gardener's Receipt Book, 1861

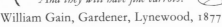

Lettuce – Sow successions of the White Paris Cos, also Malta, and Neapolitan Cabbage lettuces; transplant from seed-beds; tie up for blanching such plants as require this to be done.

Harry In my young days, tying Cos lettuce was a much used practice, mainly because most varieties of Cos were very open at the top, so the inside leaves kept grass green. But when tied they made a nice yellowish green centre, very sweet and tender. Today's Cos lettuce folds over at the top naturally and helps to blanch its centre without the need to tie.

Basil – Plant out in rich warm soil. *Sweet Marjoram* – Plant out on a south border. *Rampion* – Sow about the end of the month, on a shady border of rich earth. *New Zealand Spinach* – Plant out in the end of the month. *Tomatoes* – Plant out against a wall in the end of the month.

Cherries – Give plenty of air, but water sparingly as the fruit approaches maturity. When the fruit is gathered, remove the trees, and attend well to their being frequently syringed, and regularly watered.

Harry The cherries they're talking about are obviously planted in pots placed inside an orchard house. That's something you don't see today. Many fruit trees were grown in pots right up until the last War. I had a small collection at Chilton until the late 1950s. It was a very interesting way of growing fruit.

A Cure for Sprains

Bruise a handful of sage-leaves and boil them in a gill of vinegar for five minutes; apply this in a folded napkin as hot as it can be borne to the part affected.

Housekeeper's & Butler's Assistant, 1862

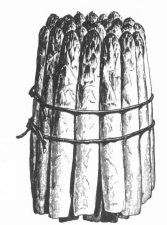

ASPARAGUS – It is a pretty name, but it does not tell us much. We have banished asparagus from the British pharmacopoeia, but the French still hold to it – chiefly, however, making use of the root. It is supposed to still and soothe the action of the heart, like foxglove; it is also supposed to act as a lithic in preventing gravel; and it is known to have a marked and very rapid action on the kidneys.

Kettner's Book of the Table, 1877

JUNE

*Fruit is gold in the morning, silver
at noon, and copper at night'. If you want to enjoy strawberries and cream to the full,
without suffering from the indulgence, have them with or after your coffee for breakfast.*
The Villa Gardener, 1870

In former months, protection from severe cold was necessary; but
now the effects of excessively hot and dry weather have to be guarded
against. Watering becomes an important operation, but recourse
should not be had to it in the open ground, so long as the health of
the plants is not endangered.

Harry June's a 'looking after what you've got' month. Even with the
weather warmed up, there were some establishments where heat was kept
on in the glasshouses. I remember that at Stansted Park the heat was never
turned off in the vineries. They wouldn't have thought we had any work
to do if there wasn't a fire to stoke! But what a difference it made to the
fruit. I'll never forget the fruit houses of those bygone days.

Beans – In the beginning of the month, a crop of the Early Long-
pod should be sown; and about the end, the latest main crop may
be put in. Earth up and top advancing crops.

Harry Plant the beans a foot apart either way, and water well like celery.
Earthing and topping up advancing crops helps to stop blackfly.

Cauliflowers – Plant out successions. Do not allow the plants to suffer
from drought; protect heads with leaves.

Small salading – Sow *cresses* and *mustard*, and other small salad seed,
at least once every week or fortnight. These seeds must now be sown
in a shady border, or otherwise shaded with mats on hot sunny days;
and the places where they are sown should be often refreshed in dry
weather with water; and this should be practised both before and
after the plants begin to appear.

Notes

_____

_____

_____

_____

_____

_____

_____

_____

_____

_____

_____

_____

_____

Potatoes – Earth up.

Harry Potatoes need regular hoeing in the early stages, and earthing up should take place when the haulm is about 9 inches high – of course, no further hoeing can then take place. Spray two or three times from late June till August with a copper compound. If disease shows up anywhere after mid August, cut off the tops immediately and lift as soon as possible.

Never place diseased tubers in the store, as they will quickly spoil your harvest. Protect from frost in the store, also cover up to keep the light away from the tubers. Otherwise many will go green and be useless for eating.

If two or three varieties are grown, make sure to label the varieties placed in store and use according to season.

Plant *pot-herbs* and other aromatic plants. Plant out from the seed-bed, but let it be done, if possible, in a showery time. Prepare some beds for that purpose, three feet and a half broad; rake the surface smooth, and then put in the plants. Plant them by line; setting them six or eight inches asunder every way, and water them. Or some of these plants may be occasionally planted in edgings, along the sides of any particular beds or border, &c., such as thyme, savory, sweet marjoram, and hyssop.
Plant out also the borage, burnet, sorrel, clary, marigold, angelica, and carduus, and all other pot and physical herbs that were sown in the spring or last autumn.

Towards the middle or latter end of the month you may sow a moderate portion of the Large Black or Spanish Turnip-rooted *radish*, to draw in August and September.

Plant out *cardoons* into the place where they are to remain to blanch. These plants must be allowed a considerable space of room to grow, in order that they may be conveniently earthed up to the proper height . . . allow the rows a yard and a half distance, and the plants three feet and a half from one another in the row.

Celeriac – Plant out, but not in trenches, in tolerably rich sandy soil.

Harry Celeriac is planted on the flat on a plot which has been well manured. Keep well watered, also feed with liquid cow-manure water as the roots begin to swell into bulbs. Only approximately half of the foliage is needed, which of course would be the top crown of leaves, so remove the rest to let air through the bed.

Cucumber – Sow or plant in ridges for pickling.

Harry Ridge cucumbers are really best raised under glass in 3-inch pots, one seed per pot. When hardened off, plant them on well-prepared ground or a piece of ground well prepared for a previous year's crop. They usually require no stopping but do benefit from waterings in dry weather. Cut regularly, otherwise the crop will rapidly fall off if the fruits are allowed to get old and seedy.

Turnips – Now sow a full crop of turnips for autumn use. The seed may be sown any time in this month, but some time between the tenth and twenty-fifth of the month is the best time to sow the principal autumn crop. However, let the seed be sown, if possible, in a dripping time, at least, when there is a prospect of rain falling soon, or immediately after. Take good care to sow this seed equally, and moderately thin, tread it down evenly, and rake it in immediately.

Harry Thin seedlings early to 4 inches apart. Sowings can continue up until July 29th. A sowing in September of Green Top Stone is useful for leaving in the ground over winter and providing greens in the spring.

Asparagus – It is advisable to terminate the general cutting for the year soon after the twentieth or twenty-fourth of the month, otherwise it will weaken the roots; for so long as you continue to cut the produce, the roots continue sending up new shoots, though every time smaller; and if continued late in the season, would greatly exhaust themselves so that the future produce next year, &c., would be diminished.

Harry Keep asparagus well watered in hot, dry weather. Liquid cow-manure water is good. I'd say finish cutting by June 17th. From June onwards watch out for the asparagus beetle. As soon as you see it, spray with malathion.

To Destroy Caterpillars on Gooseberry Trees, &c. – Get a quantity of elder leaves, and boil them in as much water as will cover them, until the liquor becomes quite black, then clear and cool it, and to every gallon of this liquor add one gallon of tobacco water. When the trees are quite dry lay it on with a fine rose waterpot, and in ten minutes the caterpillars will fall off.

To Protect Carnations, &c., from Rabbits. – Beds of carnations, picotees, pinks, and many other sorts of plants may be protected from rabbits, by simply sticking a few sticks that have been dipped in brimstone round the outside of the plants or beds. Congreve matches will, in many instances, answer the purpose; the smell is very offensive to rabbits, and they will not come near them.

To Protect Lettuce and Strawberry-beds from Snails. – If the beds are surrounded by a slate or board edging, made to stand five inches above the ground, and occasionally coated with a paste made of train oil and soot, it will form a barrier over which snails will not pass.

Do not be afraid of the weeds, but cut away. They must either be your master, or you theirs.

Everyman His Own Gardener, 1845

Where new plantations of *strawberries* are wanted, it will, about the middle or latter end of the month, be a proper time to provide some young plants for that purpose.

Harry Late June and early July is a good time to plant the young strawberry bed. From this planting a reasonable crop can be had the following year.

Much cold water applied to the roots of trees growing in them will stop the swelling of the fruit, and cause it to crack.

Harry At Chilton, just as the plums were ripening, a thunderstorm broke and we lost them all through cracking. That's happened two years running!

Pear trees on walls should have their foreright shoots pinched or cut back to six inches, always commencing at the upper part of the tree, at least a week before the lower part is interfered with, so as to check the growth, and consequently the flow of sap to the upper part. The same principle should be acted upon in the case of the apple, plum and cherry; and not only as regards those on walls, but likewise those trained as espaliers.

Harry Keeps them even.

Box Edging

Cut box edgings: the beginning or middle of the month is the proper time to begin that work. It should be done in moist weather, or soon after rain, otherwise, if cut in hot dry weather, they are apt to become brown and unsightly.

These edgings should be cut very neat, even at top, and both sides; and should not be suffered to grow higher than two or three inches, nor broader than two.

Where the edgings of box are kept to near that size, they look exceedingly neat; but where permitted to grow four, five, or six inches in height and perhaps near as much in breadth, they then have a very clumsy appearance, and make the beds and borders appear low and hollow.

A Cure for Warts

The bruised leaves of the *calendula officinalis* mixed with a few drops of reduced vinegar.

Housekeeper's & Butler's Assistant, 1862

JULY

The month of July is the hottest of all . . .
A period of rainy weather usually occurs about the middle of the month, accompanied
by thunderstorms, and this has given rise to the popular tradition respecting St
Swithin, who is supposed to baptise the apples in these rainy days.
Beeton's Shilling Gardening, 1874

Harry Round about the 29th of this month is the last day you can expect to sow anything and get it in the same year. It's worth a try with carrots, lettuce, beetroot and an early variety of broad bean and dwarf early peas. Also make the last sowing of round prickly spinach, radish and turnips.

> In the general crops of *cauliflowers* some will be still in good perfection,
> but do not require any particular care, only to break down some of
> the large leaves over the advancing flower heads to preserve them
> from the sun, rains, &c. close and firm, and in their white colour, &c.

Harry I prefer breaking the leaves over the heads rather than tying-up, because tying causes the curd to lift instead of remaining solid. It's also simpler to lift a bent-over leaf to see what the curd is doing than to untie strings.

> Sow, where required, the different sorts of small *salad herbs*; such as
> cresses, mustard, radish, &c. Where these small herbs are daily
> wanted, there should, in order to have a constant supply of such as
> are young, be some seed sown at least once every six or seven days.
> This seed must either still be sown in a shady border, or shaded from
> the sun; sow them in drills; and in dry weather daily watered, otherwise
> the plants will not come up regularly.

Harry At Stansted Park we used to sow radishes every fortnight. Fresh beds were made in April/May time. If you've got a cold frame available, it's worth having a go as well at getting young carrots and turnips. Carrots should be the Early Horn variety. They won't make anything very big but will be very acceptable in October, or even at Christmas around the turkey!

Gather mint and balm, pennyroyal, sweet-marjoram, as also carduus, hyssop , sage-tops, lavender-spikes, marigolds, and camomile flowers; and other aromatics which are now advancing towards flowering, in order to dry, to serve the family in winter.

Likewise gather spear-mint, peppermint, pennyroyal, lavender flowers, and other herbs to distil.

In early wall-trees, having fruit beginning to ripen, towards the middle or latter end of this month, hang up some phials filled with sugared water or beer, &c., in order to catch and destroy wasps, and other devouring insects, before they begin to attack the choice ripening fruit.

Let at least three such phials be placed in each of the largest trees; and in the lesser trees not less than two; and this would be more particularly expedient this or next month, in the early apricot, peach, and nectarine trees, and such like choice kinds; for the insects which generally begin to swarm about the ripening fruit of wall-trees, will, by the smell of the liquor, be decoyed into the phials and drowned.

Transplant also a full crop of *broccoli*. The plants must now be planted where they are to remain; and for that purpose dig a piece of the best ground; and if previously dunged, it will be of greater advantage to the crops.

Harry At this time of year you'd be planting out the broccoli sown in late June, early July. It would be the old May Queen type which will overwinter and turn in (head) with the turn of the days in March and April, the curd more yellow than white.

Transplant *leeks* – Choose a piece of good ground, and it will be an advantage to the plants to dig in some mellow rotten dung.

Harry If you've got empty ground, yes, transplant some leeks, because the earliest and main crop run to seed as soon as the days lengthen and they get a pipe running up through the middle, which cooks don't appreciate! Planting out now, you'll still have a complete leek – albeit only as big as your finger.

Sow some *onions* to stand the winter. This must be done in the last week of the month, and not before. But the principal sowing, is directed in next month; though it is proper to sow a few now, to afford some to draw also in autumn and beginning of winter; and may sow both of the common and the Welsh onion; the latter stands the severest frost.

Harry Some of the old boys sowed Tripoli onions in July and left them in rows to overwinter. They transplanted some in March, and it was their earliest bulb onion. Nowadays you can buy Japanese-bred onions like Senshuyu and Kaizuka which can be sown late in August and left in rows during the winter. The old Welsh onion is useful. My old uncle, who was head gardener to the Earl of Selborne, always had clumps of Welsh onion about the garden.

Now get ready some ground to sow some winter *spinach*, the latter end of this month or beginning of August. The best sort to sow for this crop is the prickly-seeded or triangular-leaved spinach, this being generally the hardiest to endure the cold and wet in winter.

Harry I think it's best to sow spinach in late June, because if you had a run on it in August you could pick it over, even though it had been sown for winter, and then it could be left alone in September so that by October you'd have ample supplies to see you through until Christmas. After Christmas, of course, it depends on the weather. Spinach used to be very popular, and I've known gardens which had to have spinach all the year round. They managed that by using frames and cloches as protection.

—— THE TEMPERATURE towards the end of last week fell considerably, and the nights were quite cold in the neighbourhood of London. In several districts hail fell, or rather showers of ice. At Kensington on the 5th inst. hailstones were scraped up by handfuls, and 'snowballing' was indulged in as a novel sport in July. At Swanley in Kent the hail did considerable damage on the 6th inst. in Mr Cannell's nursery. Dahlias were cut into tatters, and Geraniums and other flowers we noticed in a miserable state. Where the lights were left open in the Geranium house the ice shower cut quite through the foliage of the plants in the house, and of course destroyed the flowers.

Journal of Horticulture and Cottage Gardener, July 1877

Geranium Leaves – It is not generally known that leaves of the geranium are an excellent application for cuts, where the skin is rubbed off, and other wounds of that kind. One or two leaves must be bruised and applied to the part, and the cut will be cicatrised in a very short time.

Now prepare such pieces of ground as are vacant, in order to receive such seeds and plants as are proper to supply the table with necessary productions in autumn and winter.

Get ready in particular, some good ground, to plant out a principal crop of *Savoys* and *winter cabbages*. Let an open spot of ground be chosen for these plants; and let it be properly dug, and immediately put in the plants. Let them be planted in rows two feet asunder, which at this season will be room enough, except for the large kind of cabbages, which should be planted two feet and a half distance each way. A watering at planting will greatly promote the fresh rooting of all these plants.

Harry In the old days the Savoys and cabbages had a tremendous ring of guard leaves with only a small head in the middle. That's why the old books say plant up to $2\frac{1}{2}$ feet apart. Today they're more compact and you can plant them 20 inches apart in rows which are 24 inches apart.

There is one old cabbage which, if you can get hold of it, will need a lot of space, and that's the flat pole cow cabbage. I know it used to be grown a lot up to the last War. It was useful if you had staff to feed, and the other benefit was that the large leaves stifled weeds.

Kidney-beans – A late crop of either the dwarf or running kinds may still be planted . . . and more about the middle and latter end of the month of the dwarf kinds, to continue the succession of beans in gathering till Michaelmas and longer.

Harry With the autumns we've had lately, the beans wouldn't come to anything! But with an early July sowing and a mild autumn, it might be worth it!

If you've got empty frames with a growing height of 18 to 20 inches standing empty in early July, a better plan would be to sow these up with dwarf beans. Then, if frost threatens in early October, the glass lights can be put on the frames for protection.

Watering should at this time be duly practised in dry weather, to all such plants as have been lately planted out; till they have taken root; likewise to seed-beds lately sown, and where small young seedling plants are advancing.

This work should generally, at this season, in sunny weather, be done in a morning or towards the evening. The proper hours, in a morning, any time between sun-rising and eight or nine o'clock; and between the hours of four and eight or nine, in an evening; as the watering at these times has greater effect, by the moisture having time to settle gradually into the earth, before much exhaled by the great power of the full mid-day sun.

Harry In my uncle's time, men would go back and water the flower borders in the evening. Holidays at that time were virtually non-existent. You might, if you were lucky, get a week. So men did certain overtime jobs to add to their holidays. I remember this was how the man who taught me grape thinning managed to stretch his holidays.

July can certainly be very dry, and watering can be quite a problem needing much attention, especially to wall fruits. If they suffer, the fruit buds for next year are seriously affected. Without sufficient water, celery will be very stringy, runner beans will not set, late-sown seeds cannot germinate, and transplanting of leeks, brassicas, strawberries, etc. becomes a nightmare.

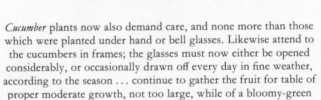

Cucumber plants now also demand care, and none more than those which were planted under hand or bell glasses. Likewise attend to the cucumbers in frames; the glasses must now either be opened considerably, or occasionally drawn off every day in fine weather, according to the season ... continue to gather the fruit for table of proper moderate growth, not too large, while of a bloomy-green colour, four or five to six or seven inches long.

Harry It pays to keep the crop cut over, because if a few start going to seed the rest of the crop soon deteriorates. It's the same for runner beans, dwarf beans, marrows and courgettes. You can't expect them to carry a seed crop and cutting crop at the same time.

——— WATER ———

The gardener who hath a full supply of water and ample means for its
distribution among his parched crops in this hot weather is a man in
the enjoyment of great privileges; let him be thankful and murmur not
because he lacketh other things which are as trifles in comparison. Do
you not agree with me, brother blue-aprons?

Journal of Horticulture, 1877

PATENT WATER BRINGER.

HAYNES AND SONS' PATENT
WATER BRINGER,
price 21s.
This simple Machine will draw
water from a pond or well 10 feet
below the level of garden, and
100 feet over the surface, with the
Hydronette or any other Garden
Engine.

THE HYDRONETTE
(ROBIN'S PATENT),

For Gardens, Greenhouses,
Conservatories, Hotbeds, Wash-
ing Windows, Carriages, &c.
Unrivalled ease of action, sim-
plicity, convenience, and force.
The HYDRONETTE is a more
useful, easy-working, reliable, and
convenient water-throwing machine than any other in use. It is
made in five sizes, viz. :—No. 1,
with 4 feet of Suction Hose,
Strainer, Jet and Rose, 12s. 6d.;
No. 2, 15s. 6d.; No. 3, £1 1s.;
No. 4, £1 5s.; No. 5, £1 10s.
Extra Hose and Union Joints to
order.

Budding Fruit Trees – Budding may now be performed in apricots, peaches, and nectarines, plums, cherries, pears and apples any time in this month in most sorts; but the general principal budding may be performed successfully any time from the middle of this to near that of next month at farthest.

Gather *seeds* of all sorts according as they ripen. Let this be done always in perfectly dry weather, cutting or pulling up the stems with the seeds thereon, and dispose them spreadingly in some airy place where the full air and power of the sun have free access, in order to dry and harden the seed in a proper degree; observing to turn them now and then; and when they have lain a few days, or a week, or a fortnight, according to the nature of the different sorts, the seed should then be beaten out, and well cleaned from the husks and rubbish, and put up in boxes or bags.

Harry Seed gathering is always interesting and often cost-saving – and, in the case of something rare, such as the old Ne plus ultra pea, the only way of saving it.

Scorzonera and *Salsify* – thin, and break off flower stems as they form.

Harry Once salsify and scorzonera throw a flower stem, the root won't retain flavour because it'll have a hard middle up through it. Rather than break the flower stem off, it's better to pull the root up altogether.

Endive – Plant out now to supply the table in autumn, a parcel of the strongest endive.... Sow in the middle and end of the month for the principal winter crops.

Harry The last week in July is the last chance for endive. It's safest to put it in a cold frame, and then in October or early November lift it and put it into a forcing shed – especially the curly-leaved kind, as a frost in October will soon touch it.

ℐotes

To Grow Names on Wall Fruit

Cut some small pieces of paper in the shapes of letters, or anything
else you please, and paste them on peaches and nectarines with
gum, just before they begin to turn colour. This should always
be pasted on the side that is most exposed to the sun; it will not
retard the swelling or deteriorate the flavour of the fruit; and
when it is ripe, it should be taken off, and it will leave the exact
print on the fruit.

The Gardener's Receipt Book, 1861

GOOSEBERRIES

The Scotch, it must be remembered,
are great in gooseberries. It is a north-
ern fruit. When there was not a tree nor
a shrub to be found in the Shetland
islands and the Orkneys, there were
gooseberry bushes in abundance; and it
was an old joke against the Shetlanders,
that when they read their Bibles and
tried to picture to themselves Adam
hiding among the trees of the garden,
they could only call up in vision a naked
man cowering under a grosart bush.

Kettner's Book of the Table, 1877

Cucumbers – Water those planted on ridges, and for pickling, with water not colder than 60 to 65°F. Therefore, spring water should not be employed till it has been exposed in tubs to the heat of the sun, or otherwise raised to the proper temperature.

Harry It used to be the practice to use warm water not only on cucumbers but on a variety of greenhouse plants as well, for example, orchids and begonias. But in the war years, with staff gone, it wasn't practical to go to the trouble of fetching warm water and they used what water was to hand. Cold water didn't seem to affect the crops, so even after the War no one bothered to go back to using warm water.

Brussels sprouts – Plant out principal crops for winter use.

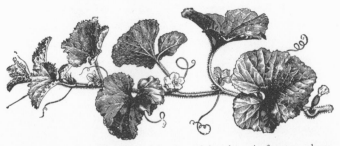

Melons – Take care now, in particular, of the plants in frames, whose fruit is beginning to ripen. These must now be allowed a large share of fresh air every day; and occasionally shaded in hot sunny weather; but where the fruit is ripening give very little water, for much moisture would spoil the flavour; however, in very hot, dry weather, the melon plants will require to be, at times, moderately watered, less or more, according to the nature and depth of earth upon the beds.

Harry My first experience of melons was growing them in frames on hot manure, the horse manure coming direct from the estate farm. You got good melons, but they needed a lot of labour and attention.

Under good cultivation melons will take a lot of sun. I wouldn't shade them (except when first planted) but would give them some air when the temperature rises over 75°F, and keep the surrounds damp. As soon as the sun goes in or the temperature drops, damp down and close the frame or house. Cantaloupes are the sort most people grow today. They can be sown in a warm house (60°F) in early May so that you can have a plant to put out in late May or early June. You need to plant them about a yard apart.

NOTES

_____
_____
_____
_____
_____
_____
_____
_____
_____
_____
_____
_____
_____
_____
_____

Artichokes will now be advancing fast to perfection in full-grown heads which, and the plants together, may be assisted in their present and future growth, by a little occasional culture. On this occasion, it may be proper to intimate, that if desirous to have large full-sized artichokes, to encourage the principal to head, cut off most of the lower small ones or side suckers, in their young growth, or the size of large eggs; and these, in some families, are also prepared for the table.

The maturity of full-grown artichokes in perfection for the table is generally apparent by the scales of the head opening detachedly asunder, and before the flowers appear in the centre.

Likewise, observe generally, that according as all the full-grown artichokes on each stem are gathered for the table, to cut or break down the stems close to the ground, which, in some degree, encourages a bottom growth more effectually, in forming strong new shoots against winter.

Harry It was always the practice to cut the tops of artichokes because the old boys used to think they were an eyesore. Of course, it also encourages buds to make shoots from the base for the following year.

Landing-up celery – Land or earth up the crop of early celery planted into trenches last month, or in May; break the earth moderately well with a hoe or spade, and trim it up neatly to both sides of the rows of plants; three or four inches high, repeating the earthing at this time about once a week to have some blanched as early as possible.

Lettuce – Dig also a spot of the best mellow ground, and sow some lettuce-seed: the Cos, Cilicia, imperials, large, white and brown Dutch cabbage-lettuces or some of each are still the most proper kinds.

Harry Remember that when you thin out your row of lettuce, the best of the thinnings are worth planting because they'll come ten days later and give a succession from one sowing. Lettuce sown late this month will head in late September, early October, and be quite useful.

AUGUST

*Less rain falls this month than in July,
according to the ordinary course of Nature, and the mean temperature is a little higher
than in that month, the nights being certainly hotter.*
Beeton's Shilling Gardening, 1874

Harry August is one of the quietest months in the garden. It's too late to plant much out and too late to sow. It's a time for attention to detail, collecting the crops that have matured, and watering such crops as celery, cardoons and celeriac. If you're growing strawberries in pots under glass, they can now be potted into their final big pots and stood out onto a base of ashes before being taken in again in December. This method should give you strawberries in April.

Bulbs for the earliest forcing, such as hyacinths, daffodils, irises and tulips, can be potted up and plunged into ashes or leaf soil and left for eight weeks. In days gone by, inside staff below foremen often had to wait for their holidays, only being allowed to take them after the bulb potting and the final potting of strawberries were complete.

Propagate, where wanted, the different sorts of *aromatic plants*; the slips or cuttings of the branch shoots of many sorts may still be planted, and will grow; but where any admit of slipping from the bottom with roots, it will be more successful.
Particularly the slips of sage, hyssop, winter-savory, and marjoram, will still succeed, but must be planted in the beginning of the month. Let the slips or cuttings be about 5, 6 or 7 inches long, planted in a shady border, and in dry weather duly water them, and also plant in the beginning of the month slips of lavender, rue, rosemary, wormwood, and southernwood.

Every *weed* that is suffered to stand to scatter its seeds upon the ground lays the foundations of hundreds in the year to come.

Harry One year's seed is seven years' weed! Take every chance to weed in August and September. It's difficult to kill weeds by hoeing later than August because the sun loses power and won't kill the weeds if they're lying on top of the ground, especially after a shower of rain. It's still good advice to follow the old adage and hoe even when the weeds aren't visible.

Peach and nectarine trees should have a number of dry bean-stalks introduced among the branches to trap earwigs. Go over these every morning and blow the insects out of the bean-stalks into a bottle half filled with water; replace the stalks, and continue till the insects are reduced to few or none.

The Gardener's Assistant, 1859

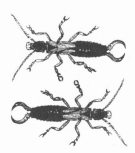

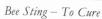

Bee Sting – To Cure

Immediately after taking out the sting, get an onion and bruise it, and apply it to the stung place, and it will afford immediately relief.

The Gardener's Receipt Book, 1861

Get ready some ground, where it was not done last month, to sow a
good crop of winter and spring *onions*.
This being the most eligible season to sow the general crop to draw
in young growth for winter and spring service, and some for early
heading summer onions, must be done in the first, but at the farthest
the second week in the month; and for that purpose choose a clean
dry-lying spot; and when the ground is digged, mark out beds three
feet and a half, or four feet broad; then sow the seed tolerably thick,
in a regular manner; then tread it in, and rake the ground evenly, that
the seed may be equally covered, and the plants rise regularly in every
part of the bed.

Harry I'd sow winter and spring onions at the *end* of August. Scuff the
seed in with your feet if the soil is reasonably dry and walk up the drill.
Then, draw the rake over in the same direction as the run of the drills.

<hr />

The *gathering of various fruits* will require particular attention in this
month. Early kinds of apples and pears, if gathered a few days too
early, will be watery and insipid; and will not become sugary by lying
in the fruit-room. If, on the other hand, they are allowed to remain
a few days longer on the tree than they ought to do, they become
mealy. Their precise period of maturity must therefore be watched.
Apples and pears ripening at this time should not be gathered during
the hot period of the day, otherwise they are apt to turn sour.
Gooseberries, currants, raspberries, and strawberries, are best
gathered when cool and dry; but peaches, nectarines, apricots, plums,
and cherries, may be gathered when dry at any time of the day.

Harry Early apples and pears have a short shelf life. Keswick Codling,
Warner's King and other old cookers, left on the trees too late, rapidly lose
all flavour. Early dessert apples such as Beauty of Bath and Irish Peach are
completely useless if you pick them too soon, and if you pick them just
right but keep them a day or two too long in the fruit room, they're also
useless! The best way to judge the time to pick, is to watch until a few
apples fall off, then as a rule it's time to clear the whole crop. It's usual to
use early cookers straight from the tree and not attempt to store them.

$$\mathcal{N}\text{OTES}$$

_____
_____
_____
_____
_____
_____
_____
_____
_____
_____
_____
_____
_____
_____
_____

TOMATO OR LOVE APPLE.

It appears according to the 'Hortus Kewensis' to have been cultivated in England as early as 1596, and Gerarde mentions it in his work, which was published in 1597, as growing in his garden. Parkinson, whose works were published in 1656, mentions it as being cultivated in England for ornament and curiosity only. For a long time, however, it has been grown for use as well as for ornament, and is increasing in esteem yearly. In America it is extensively cultivated, and much attention has been given there to the raising of improved varieties. Some of these have already become popular in England, such as Hathaway's Excelsior, The Trophy, and some others, which are remarkable for their smoothness and general good quality.

The most recent of the American varieties – namely, Vick's Criterion Tomato, has been awarded a first-class certificate by the Royal Horticultural Society. This beautiful variety was raised by Mr James Vick, the well-known seed grower of New York. It is a very prolific well-shaped variety with smooth skin, very distinct in colour, the fruit being of a cornelian red. The seed has been placed in the hands of Messrs. James Carter & Co. for distribution.

Journal of Horticulture, 1877

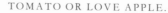

Asparagus – Let the plantations be well watered and kept at this time perfectly free from weeds; in particular that which was planted in beds last March or April.

Wall-trees still demand attention; particularly peaches, nectarines, and such like this.
Let them be once more carefully looked over, and see whether all the branches and shoots remain secure in their proper places. Where any have been displaced by winds or other accidents, let them be nailed up again in a secure and neat manner; and where any of the shoots are loose, or project considerably from the wall, or have extended in length, let the whole be nailed in close and securely.

Harry Nails and tag were the earliest form of keeping fruit trees on the walls and in some gardens, including here at Chilton, this was the method used up until the end of the last War. The tag was made from old clothes, torn up into strips approximately an inch wide and rolled up into balls the size of a ball of knitting wool. The nails were specially made. They were 4-sided, about $1\frac{1}{2}$ inches long and ended in a hard point which could be driven into brick or mortar. A piece of cloth was cut off, long enough to go around the branch or twig with an inch to spare on either end, and the nail driven through the two ends. Large branches would have these supports every 12 inches along.

It was a slow and often very cold job. In large gardens men often followed the winter sun around as the day wore on, sometimes moving two or three times a day to warm vantage points in the garden. Another practice for keeping warm at least in a Scottish garden I heard about, was to have a piece of digging started where the nailing and pruning was going on, so that when the men got cold they did a bit of digging and then went back to the pruning!

In the gardens at Chilton it used to take two men from the end of October till very often mid March to complete tag and nailing, and they needed several winters of training to become really good at it. With the cost of labour today, the old method is out of the question. Now trees on walls are tied to wires – much quicker and far, far easier.

Go over the stocks or trees which were budded in July, and let all the bandages be loosened.

Harry If the bud has taken, the 'strig' on the piece you've budded will fall off. If you see that the bud has swollen, it's quite safe to release the bast ties around the bandages.

There are now available more modern devices than bandages to help you bud. Some are like pieces of elastic secured with two staples. The material on these rots as the bud swells, so there's no need to take them off.

74

Raspberries – Thin the young shoots, leaving from four to six of the strongest. After the crop is gathered from the bearing branches, they should be cut, so that the young shoots for bearing next summer may have all the light and nourishment.

Harry Prune out the old fruiting wood as soon as the crop has been cleared. Tie in the new canes 6 inches apart, selecting the strongest then cutting out all others to ground level.

Continue to sow, in succession, several sorts of small *salad seeds*, such as mustard, cresses, radish, rape and turnip. Let them be sown in a shady border, or where they may be occasionally shaded with mats, from the mid-day sun, till the plants come up. . . . This is now a good time to sow the seeds of corn-salad, or otherwise lamb-lettuce, for winter and spring service; and also the seeds of chervil for the same occasion.

Harry It's alright to sow mustard, cress, radish and rape, but it's too late to make a bulb of turnip. You would probably get a thick root in place of a bulb and a rosette of leaves. It might make useful turnip greens in the spring, although they'd be somewhat strong in flavour, certainly stronger than sprouting broccoli or sprout or cabbage greens.

Cardoons – Those which were planted out in June will now be arrived to some considerable height; and it will be proper to begin to tie up some, and land up some earth round the plants, in order to blanch or whiten them, and render the stalks of the leaves crisp, tender, and mild-tasted for use; and, as they rise in height, let the earthing be accordingly repeated.

Sow early and other *cabbage* seed, to produce plants for the service of next summer. Also sow the large autumn kinds to succeed the summer crops, and for autumn and winter supply the following year. But this early seed must not be sown until some time between the 6th and the 12th of the month; nor must it be sown later, there being an advantage in sowing it just at that time; for was the seed to be sown sooner, many of the plants would be apt to run to seed in March; and was it to be sown later in the month, the plants would not get proper strength before winter.

Harry Early and other cabbage is usually sown nowadays in the last week in July or up to the first 12 days of August.

The great difficulty of this month is want of room. Therefore, make all the clearance you can by completing your stock of pickles, preserves, and dried herbs.

Artichokes will be in perfection this month, and should be cut for use as soon as the scales of the head expand, and before they open in the heart for flowering.

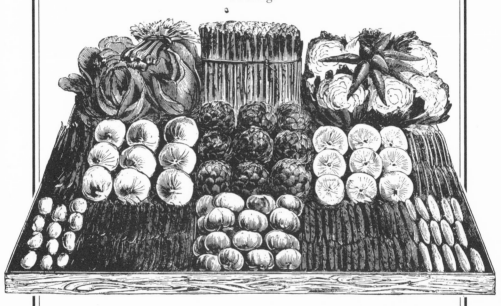

When the Englishman, still more the Englishwoman, determines that a salad is not to be eaten with salt alone, but must be bathed in some mixture, one discovers a curious weakness in the national taste – a chariness of oil, and love of vinegar. An odd proof of this is to be found in the scientific nomenclature of the gardeners. Like all sciolists, they are fond of inventing new names. They are not content to call salad-plants, as of old, salad-plants, – that is, plants to be eaten with salt; they have invented the name of acetarious plants, – that is, plants to be eaten with vinegar. There is the true English idea – a salad is the infancy of mixed pickles. We have a besotted love of pickles in England, and never seem to understand that vinegar in a salad must be doled out with a niggardly hand.

Kettner's Book of the Table, 1877

Sowing Lettuce-Seed, and Order of Transplanting

Sow lettuce-seed, at two different times this month, for use both this autumn, and the following winter and spring.

The first sowing is to be performed some time before the tenth of the month, and is to raise plants for supplying the table in September, October, and November &c.; the second sowing must be done some time between the fifteenth and twenty-first of the month; and the plants raised from this sowing are some to be planted out in September and October for winter supply; and in others, such as Cilicia, brown Dutch, common white, and hardy green cabbage lettuce, to be both transplanted into beds or borders, and a principal supply remain where sown, and thinned moderately to cut for use, thinningly, as wanted in winter or spring; and a good quantity of the Cos and other lettuces to be planted out in September and October upon warm borders, in order to stand the winter, to supply the table next March, April and May.

Harry Years ago they weren't blessed with such reliable lettuce cultivars as we have today. Many failed to make really good heads, just a rosette of leaves, but, of course, it got them by. I can remember my old uncle in the autumn sowing lettuce thinly in boxes made for the job. The boxes were 2 by 1½ feet and 4 or 5 inches deep – and put into the flowering houses. He allowed the lettuce to grow and then cut it off down to soil level. Of course, it was only leaves, but apparently it satisfied the cook up at the kitchens.

Bulbing Keeping Onions – Examine the main crops of bulbing onions; they will now in general be fully bulbed towards the middle of this month; when their stalks and leaves begin to fall and wither, the roots have had their full growth, and must then be taken up. Let this be done in dry weather and as you take them up pull off the gross part of the stalks and leaves, only observing to leave to each onion about three or four inches of stalk.

Harry Early in July I turn the foliage from one onion into the foliage of the one in the next row. After 10 days or a fortnight there's not much leaf left on them. This also helps the ripening process. When I lift the onions I put them in an airy vinery or frame.

Cherry and Plum Stones
Preserve cherry and plum stones, &c., for sowing to raise
stocks for budding and grafting.

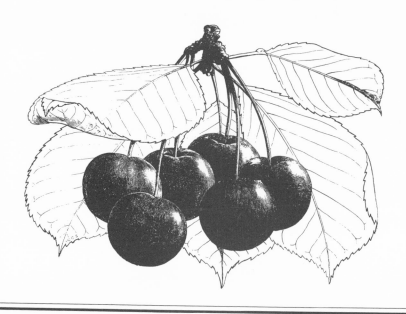

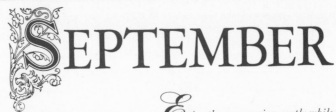

SEPTEMBER

Enjoy the summer innocently while it lasts.
Treat your master well, if you happen to be a servant; treat your servant well, if
Providence has made you a master. Be thankful to Heaven for the blessings of health,
strength, and freedom: and remember that a gardener's work is never done.
The Kitchen Garden, 1859

Harry September generally gives you time to take stock of your crops, to note which ones have done well and those which haven't. Keep an eye on apples and pears. Some will need picking, so the fruit room must be made ready, and if you hope to exhibit apples and pears at the October exhibitions, the best specimens must be looked out now and afforded some sort of protection from the birds. Summer pruning can still go ahead, and anything surplus to immediate requirements should be preserved for the winter. I like to get rambler and climbing rose pruning out of the way in September, and a great joy to me this month each year is the flowering wild cyclamen. Heating equipment will soon be needed, so give it a trial run.

In the old days, chrysanthemums were grown on a large scale in pots, and these always needed lots of attention in September; tying, feeding, disbudding, keeping them clean from pests, and everything made ready under glass to receive them in October.

When I was a lad, hop picking in September bought our winter clothes and gave a bit of cash for a holiday away before returning to school.

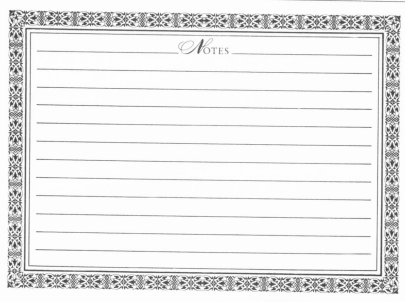

Notes

_____
_____
_____
_____
_____
_____
_____
_____
_____
_____
_____
_____
_____

When you hear the first gun pop at the unhappy partridges, remember, if you have forgotten, or been unable to do anything which ought to have been done in August, and remedy the omission before the sun goes down.

WOODLICE AND ANTS will be inclined to emigrate if their haunts and hiding-places are daily broken in upon by the hoe and rake.

Mushrooms – This is now a principal season to begin to provide
mushroom spawn and to prepare proper supplies of hot dung for
making mushroom beds, in which to plant the said spawn for the
production of mushrooms ...
Choose a dry-lying place, either in the melon ground, wherein to
make the bed, or on any other dry sheltered situation; and the bed
should be made generally wholly upon the surface of the ground. ...
Mark out on the ground the width and length of the bed, which must
be at least three and a half to four feet wide, and as long as you shall
think convenient, from fifteen or twenty to fifty feet, or more,
according to the quantity you intend to raise, and is to be made
ridgeways, like the roof of a house, about three and a half to four
feet high.
Bring in the dung, and lay the bottom of the bed to the full extent;
and as you advance in height, draw both sides in gradually from the
bottom, till you bring, as it were, to nothing at the top.
Having made the bed, you must let it remain for at least a fortnight
or three weeks, or a month, according to its substance and extent,
before you put in the spawn, or at least till the heat is becoming quite
moderate ... have two or three long sticks thrust down into the
dung, to pull up occasionally to try the heat; which be sure let be
quite mild, reduced to a very low warmth, before you venture the
spawn in: for this is very delicate, impatient both of too much heat,
severe cold, and copious moisture.

Harry I've never seen these types of beds made, and only know of the
practice from the older generation and my uncle's old books. As I see it, it
must have been a very hit and miss affair. There couldn't have been much
certainty about it and yet it was undoubtedly carried out. Something similar
was carried out in a cold but dry shed in one of my pre-War establishments.
It was placed during September or early October and cased in with maiden
soil gathered from the park from heaps raised by the moles. It kept
reasonably moist. When the winter wore on and became really cold, the
bed was covered with straw and frost never got to it. In March or April
the straw was removed, the casing soil kept moist and mushrooms appeared
in April and May.

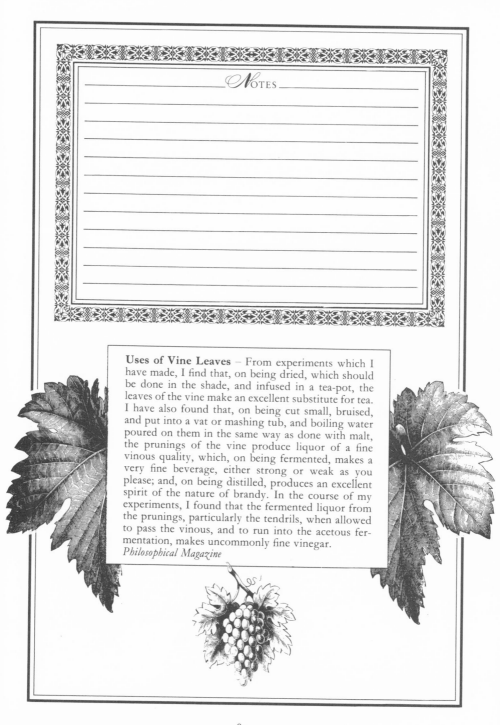

*N*OTES

Uses of Vine Leaves – From experiments which I have made, I find that, on being dried, which should be done in the shade, and infused in a tea-pot, the leaves of the vine make an excellent substitute for tea. I have also found that, on being cut small, bruised, and put into a vat or mashing tub, and boiling water poured on them in the same way as done with malt, the prunings of the vine produce liquor of a fine vinous quality, which, on being fermented, makes a very fine beverage, either strong or weak as you please; and, on being distilled, produces an excellent spirit of the nature of brandy. In the course of my experiments, I found that the fermented liquor from the prunings, particularly the tendrils, when allowed to pass the vinous, and to run into the acetous fermentation, makes uncommonly fine vinegar.
Philosophical Magazine

Tie together the leaves of *endive* to blanch the plants white, tender, and mild-tasting; observing generally to perform it in dry weather, and principally to the largest full-sized plants, of good stocky growth and full in the heart; and in doing this work, gather up the leaves evenly in your hand, and tie them together with a string of bast, or small osier twig, a little above the middle of each plant.

Hoe *turnips*; let this be done in a dry day; and let your hoe be sharp, and of a middle size.

Now begin to gather autumn *apples* and *pears* for keeping, according as they arrive to mature growth; many of the autumn sorts will be ready to take down for that purpose towards the middle or latter end of the month; but for present service, several sorts will be of eligible growth to pick here and there off the trees any time this month, occasionally as wanted.

Peaches and *nectarines* attract thousands of enemies, consisting of wasps, earwigs, flies, and ants; and in moist weather snails even will set upon the nectarines. The various insects attack in preference the best and fairest fruits. The greatest connoisseur could not better select the finest flavour.

Harry To protect grapes today some people draw a nylon stocking over them, but it has to be a pretty big stocking, and when you pull it off it takes the bloom off the grapes. The way I used to cope with a wasp problem in a house was to put tiffany netting on to all the ventilators, and when the vinery door stood open, I made a temporary door of tiffany.

Spinach – Hoe and thin. If not already done, the winter crop should be sown early in the month.

Harry Keep spinach clean this month, because there's nothing worse than going out to pick spinach on a bad winter's day and having big weeds and rubbish up through it.

In this month the protection of *ripening fruit*, and the gathering of it when it is fit, require the most urgent attention ... The leaves that shade peaches and nectarines should be turned aside, and the fruit may be exposed to the direct rays of the sun. Over some of these fruits which it is most important to preserve, Halliman's fruit protectors may be placed.

Harry The method used to preserve pears at Stansted Park was to put paper bags, slightly greased, over them so as to resist the rain. The foreman selected potential show fruits and tied them with green fillis. Ordinary fruit for the house was tied with bast. But the problem with putting bags over the fruit was that it didn't colour up! So Mr Tomalin, the head gardener at Stansted, had the fruit picked slightly before one would have picked it. The fruit was then put into trays and sunk into wood wool, and the trays were put into a cage in the green grass. The dew at night and the sun in the day brought a natural colouring up of the fruit, but you had to have great skill or it didn't look natural. The old foreman there had it down to a fine art!

In dry weather, the ground should be kept well hoed, so that not a vestige of weeds may be seen when wet sets in. There will then be less occasion to tread and puddle the ground in attempting to destroy weeds when the state of the weather is unfavourable for doing so.

Harry This is good advice. When I was a lad working at Stansted Park, I was cleaning the ground between fruit trees when it came on to rain. Instead of leaving the cleaning up and going off to another job, I kept on with it. The foreman told me that that particular bit of ground would never work right for the rest of the year, and he was right. Where I'd trod in the rain the soil had compacted, and whenever it rained again the rain never soaked straight in but puddled on the surface.

Parsley – Cut down, in order that young leaves may be formed before winter.

Harry With the autumn rains, the soft summer growth will flop over. But if you cut down a section of the row, it'll produce nice short stocky sprigs which will resist the rain.

Cucumbers – To Keep for a Length of Time Quite Fresh
When the cucumbers are at their best they should be cut, and laid in a box made for the purpose, just to fit them, and then bury the box in some dry sand, covering it over to the depth of a foot. There should not be any hay or moss put with them in the box, as it will cause them to turn yellow. If laid in the box without hay or moss their colour and bloom may be preserved for a fortnight to look as fresh as the day they were cut. Melons may also be kept in the same way. *The Gardener's Receipt Book, 1861*

Wasps' Nests – To Destroy
Procure a glass bottle of the usual size, and rinse it out with spirits of turpentine, and thrust the neck of the bottle into the hole, and stop it all round with mud, completely preventing the ingress and egress of wasps. The fumes of the turpentine will soon destroy the wasps, so that the nests may be digged out a fortnight afterwards, and they will be found dead.

OCTOBER

The eighth month from March, October, is the first month of the old Roman year, and according to quaint old Peachum 'is drawn in a garment of yellow and carnation; upon his head a garland of oak leaves, in his right hand the sign of Scorpio, and in his left a basket of "services", medlars, and other fruits that ripen late.'
Beeton's Shilling Gardening, 1874

The Gardening year may be considered as commencing with this month, both because gardens are mostly taken possession of at new or old Michaelmas, and because now is the time to lay a foundation for the coming year.

Harry October is a good time to move if you're a gardener, because it gives you a chance to see the potential of a new garden and to assess past mistakes.

This month sees the moving of many items, such as chrysanthemums (especially in days gone by) and the last of the melons. The apple and pear harvest result in that grand scent from the fruit room. In a well run garden, October marks the beginning of the winter cultivations. Somehow it is always nice to see that first piece of ground turned over. There's an easing off of watering, but the boring job of keeping the fallen leaves cleaned up remains.

It's no longer possible to go back up the gardens for a quiet look round – it's jacket on now, and torch in hand – but the thought of long evenings by the fire is comforting.

Box – Plant where wanted for edgings to borders, or beds; this being a very successful season to do that work, for the box will now very soon root.
Thrift also makes a very good edging, and this is a very proper time to plant it.

Harry Thrift planted early and favourably in October would take root for a good display in the spring. If October weather is favourable, it's a good planting month for many items, such as trees, shrubs, herbaceous plants, roses, and all manner of fruit trees.

NOTES

The gardener holds a unique and enviable position in this land of work and taxation. Where is the man who, like he, can raise his own celery every year, let alone be master of the mint?

... though he dresses plain and his only decoration is bachelor's buttons, he is always recognised, and meets with more boughs than a minister of state.

From a Victorian head gardener's album

The capital fruits designed for long keeping should all be carefully pulled one by one, and put into a basket, taking care to lay them in gently, that they may not bruise one another. According as the fruits are gathered, let them be carried into the fruitery, or some convenient, dry, clean apartment; and if room enough, it would be proper to lay them carefully in heaps, each sort by themselves.

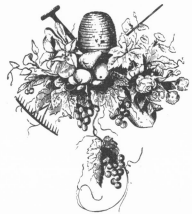

Everyman His Own Gardener, 1845

This is the time to sow *haws, holly, hips,* and *yewberries.* Beds must be prepared to these berries three feet and a half or four feet wide; the berries are to be sown each sort separate, and covered an inch or two deep with earth.
But it is the practice of many to prepare the holly-berries and haws, for vegetation, a whole year before they sow them, because they seldom come up till the second spring after sowing; it therefore is customary to bury them in the ground in a heap together, for one year, and then sow them.

Cabbage – About the middle or latter end of this month, you may plant out some of the strongest early cabbage plants, in the place where they are to remain for cabbaging early next summer.

Harry I reckon on cutting the first spring cabbage in Whitsun week, but in a favourably sited garden you can be cutting before this. On the Blackmoor estate down in Hampshire, we used to cut one for Whitsun and at the same time pick the first gooseberries.

Potatoes intended for sets may be greened in the sun.

Harry In the large kitchen gardens they used to have chitting trays to green the potatoes in. They stood on top of one another. Making them was the job of the garden's carpenter, who was a useful man to have about. In the summer he mowed and in the winter helped with the pruning and got pea and bean sticks. Because he had a 'trade' he got sixpence or ninepence a day extra. One garden's carpenter I knew also had 'sock' money – that was to pay for the socks he wore out, walking behind the mower over the seven acres he had to mow!

The *strawberry* beds should, some time in this month, have their winter dressing.
New plantations of strawberries may now be made where wanted, and this may be done any time in the month, but the sooner the better.

Harry They seemed to pay a lot of attention to strawberries in Victorian times. They'd have four or five varieties in one bed to have a succession, although some of them didn't last long. The only Victorian variety which has survived through to today is Royal Sovereign, which was brought in in 1902.
It's a useful idea to put short manure on to a strawberry bed at this time of year and let the worms and weather work it into the bed.

WANTED, as HEAD GARDENER a first-class energetic man, to take the entire management of extensive Houses and Pleasure Stove, and Greenhouse Plants. Will have nine men under him. Salary £100, with house, fuel and vegetables. Send copies of testimonials to B., Mr C. Hedgelong, Grafton Street, Dublin.

The Gardener's Record, 1870

Nasturtiums – Gather for pickling.

Harry A good idea – before the mice or frost gets them!

Now clear the beds of *aromatic plants* from weeds, and let them have the winter dressing. This must be particularly observed in the beds of sage, savory, thyme, marjoram, and hyssop; and also the beds of mint, balm, tarragon, tansy, camomile, penny-royal, burnet, and sorrel: and all other beds of aromatics, and pot-herbs.

As the *asparagus* stalks have now done growth, and the seed-berries ripe, where required to save the seed, they should at any time this month, or beginning of next, be cut down, and the beds have the proper winter dressing.

Harry Cleaned up now, the asparagus bed will be spick and span for the winter. The winter dressing of manure can be raked off next March and put in the alleyways as frost, weather and birds will pull it to pieces.

This is a good season to plant *raspberries*, where a new plantation is wanted.

You may begin planting *gooseberry* and *currant* trees about the middle or towards the latter end of the month. Where it is intended to plant these shrubs in a full plantation by themselves, allow them proper room, in rows eight or ten feet distant, and at least six feet between plant and plant in the row.

Prune *gooseberries* and *currant* about the end of this month; and the ground about them may be dug, which will render the whole decent for the winter season, and will be of great service to the trees.

Harry I'd prune blackcurrants as soon as the fruit is cleared, because they make next year's fruit on the young growth made this year. Redcurrants I'd have pruned in the summer, but if not, I would certainly get on with them now. Some people leave pruning gooseberries until March so that the unpruned growth keeps birds away from the buds.

Notes

WINTERING GERANIUMS

WHENEVER I see information given on wintering these plants I note that it is not of an encouraging kind to 'small people' like myself, and yet those are the very people who are chiefly interested. A light place would, according to our instructors, appear to be indispensable, such as a greenhouse. No doubt a greenhouse is a great advantage to a garden, and is the best place for Geraniums; but I have wintered hundreds of plants without their having been in a greenhouse, and they have proved very useful.

The plants are simply taken up in October and are divested of all the fibrous roots. The tops are also cut off, leaving not more than half an inch of the main shoots. The wood there is quite brown and hard, and is not prone to decay; at any rate, decay is prevented by dressing the wounds with dry fresh lime at the time the plants are cut down. These stumps – for stumps they are – are closely packed in boxes of moderately moist soil, which is placed firmly round the roots. By making the soil firm sufficient moisture is retained to keep the stumps fresh without watering them during the winter. If the soil is loose it speedily becomes dry, and when water is applied in winter decay succeeds.

The boxes are placed in an old building which is nearly dark and nearly frost-proof, and all that is required to preserve the Geraniums is to cover them with perfectly dry hay during severe weather. They are examined occasionally, and if there is any evidence of mould a prompt application of dry lime checks it at once.

Journal of Horticulture, 1877

You may now sow a first moderate crop of early *pease*, to have a chance of an early production next summer, in May and June, they may be sown in the middle or latter end of the month, and the produce will come in at an early season, provided they escape the frost . . . a warm south border, under a wall or other fence, is the proper situation.

Harry It would be alright to sow Meteor now.

Lettuces for the winter service, of the August or early September sowing; stout plants of the Cos, hardy, and common cabbage lettuce; brown Dutch and Cilicia kinds, should, in the beginning or middle of the month, be planted out in beds of rich, light earth, in a sheltered situation six or eight inches asunder; they will supply the table before and after Christmas.

Harry I'd prefer to put lettuce in frames at this time of year. They used to have them in frames at Ashburnham. Some of these establishments set great store by lettuce and insisted on having it all the year round, which meant having it in batches of pots all the winter. The problem always used to be that lettuce pushed out of season soon becomes infested with aphids, and it was a dickens of a job to get them off.

Prepare vacant ground for future crops. Remove all fallen and decayed leaves; and continue to hoe, weed, and stir the ground occupied by crops. Dress the herb border. Draw earth to the stems of the cabbage tribe.

Harry We used to draw earth up to the stems of Brussels sprouts and purple sprouting broccoli to give them better anchorage, but I think it was more fussy than useful. Something that also used to be done was to heel the plant away from the wind with a forkful of soil, but this must have spoilt the roots quite a bit.

Tomatoes – Gather fruit and hang up in a warm place, or lay them on a hurdle, or on wicker-work, in a frame or vinery.

KITCHEN APPLES

Most of these are called codlings – from the old verb to coddle, to boil a little, stew or simmer. The peculiar virtue of a kitchen apple is expressed in a phrase which is a constant reminder of the Garden of Eden – to fall. An apple is said to fall when on being cooked it forms a pulpy mass of equal consistence.

Kettner's Book of the Table, 1877

Winter pears and apples should in general be gathered this month. Observe, that in proceeding to gather the principal keeping fruits, both of the apples and pears, generally choose a dry day, and when the trees and fruit are also tolerably dry from about ten or eleven o'clock till three or four in the afternoon.

Celery should now be very truly earthed up according as it advances in height, in order that the plants may be well blanched a due length before severe frosts attack them.

Likewise the *cardoons* now give a general full earthing, in open dry weather, and when the leaves of the plant are dry. In earthing these plants, observe, at each time, first to tie with a hay-band their leaves close together, gathering the leaves up regularly. Then let the earth be well broken, and lay it up equally of a proper thickness, and some considerable height about every plant.

In the latter end of the month begin to dig up the main crops of full-grown *carrots*, some best *parsnips*, *potatoes* and *red beet*, &c., and such other carrot-shaped esculent roots, to preserve them in sand, to be at all times ready for winter service.

Harry They always used to reckon that potatoes had to ripen, but I prefer to have potatoes out in September. I have found they keep just as well, and digging them is more pleasant in September. To make sure of the best parsnips, take them up, but leave the rest in the ground. I'd clear all the carrots and beet because they usually get attacked by mice or pheasants, or worm gets into the carrot.

Plums, cherries, pears, and *apple* trees, upon walls and espaliers, may be pruned in the latter end of this month, provided the leaves are mostly all down.

About the end of this month you may begin to prune *peaches* and *nectarines*, if their leaves are dropped; and you may also prune and nail *apricots*.

When the leaves of *peach* and *nectarine* trees begin to fall, take a fine-twigged birch broom and lightly touch the leaves, moving the broom from the base of the branches towards their extremities. The leaves that are thus very easily removed are of no use as regards the vegetation of the tree; and by dispensing with them, more sun and air will be admitted for the better maturing the wood of the young shoots.

Harry We often used to brush leaves off the trees inside the glasshouses, because in the old days you had to keep the houses neat and tidy. Brushing leaves off the outside trees could be done if there was a spell of mild weather in October and you could get on with tying in the shoots. The leaves should have turned yellow, which indicates that they have served their purpose for the year. The best broom to use is a new besom, because the twiggy bits are quite light and won't harm buds on the trees. Another method of getting rid of leaves is to give the tree a good shake with your fist!

NOVEMBER

At this season the foliage undergoes a natural decadence, and dead leaves there will be in plenty, requiring regular and constant removal. Cleanliness and neatness should now be scrupulously carried out in conservatories, showhouses or greenhouses proper.
The Gardener's Chronicle, 1870

Harry The kitchen garden had its share of dreariness in November – manure wheeling, digging, trenching, clearing spent crop rubbish, lifting root crops could all be awful in November. One task not too bad was picking the Sturmer Pippin apples, which were allowed to hang after the leaves had left the trees. Pruning was always under way, especially Morello cherries and outside peaches and nectarines – these were tied before Christmas. Hotbed frames were cleared out in November.

One pleasant task that started in November was the beginning of the forcing. Seakale, chicory, endive (the Batavian broad leaf) and rhubarb were grown under ground in tunnel-like chambers, with the greenhouse hot-water pipes running through them, or in a dark shed near the boiler house, again with pipes running through the shed. Either place would have beds of soil and the roots of the various crops were planted in them at quite close plantings, watered in and the cockroach trays put down. *The light would be put out and the door shut* – two golden rules when it comes to forcing.

Every Friday afternoon I used to have to take a handbrush into the flowering house in the walled garden at Ashburnham. Every leaf or petal and any soil washed out of the pots had to be brushed off the staging. I've seen that flowering house staged up with lovely flowering plants and no one looked at them apart from the garden staff – but of course, it had to be done in case someone came.

In the beginning of this month you may finish planting some *cabbage* plants of the early kinds, if not done in October, to come forward next spring and summer, in April and May, &c. Choose strong good plants, and set them in rows, eighteen inches or two feet asunder.

Harry In the following March, a dressing (of 2 ounces per square yard of nitrate of soda) was usually put on and lightly hoed in. It gave the cabbages a boost and a good colour.

_____
_____
_____
_____
_____
_____
_____
_____
_____
_____
_____
_____
_____
_____

JOTTINGS ABOUT VEGETABLES

It may or may not be news, but the fact is our colliers down here are possessed of quite a craze after Leeks. I know of even 2*d.* a-piece being offered for some when in the seed pan, and every village has, independent of other shows, its Leek show. In the report I wish it to be particularly noticed that all the prizes are comprised of useful household articles, which I like; every time you see them they create pleasure. Somehow you lose sight of money; it has wings, and ere you are aware it is flown. – J. Witherspoon, Red Rose Vineries, Chester-le-Street.

PELTON FELL LEEK SHOW

A Leek Show was held at the house of Mr Thomas Mason's, Hot Hills, Pelton Fell, when a number of prizes were offered for competition. There was a good number of entries, and the Leeks shown received high commendation from all the visitors, as well as the professional gentlemen who judged them. The following were the successful competitors, and the prizes awarded to each: – For best three Leeks, Thomas Batey, a cruet stand; 2nd, John Ferguson, a coffee pot; 3rd, John Studham, a teapot; 4th, Robert Appleton, a teapot; 5th, William Wishart, a cruet stand; 6th, John Johnson, half-dozen knives and forks; 7th, John Barker, half-dozen table spoons; 8th, George Armin, pair of salts; 9th, Thomas Mason, jun., pair of candlesticks; 10th, Luke Mason, pair of butter knives; 11th, Joseph Wrangham, bread board and knife; 12th, James Dixon, pair of candlesticks; 13th, John English, a pocket knife; 14th, Matthew Wass, a set of brushes; 15th, John Hollison, a cruet stand; 16th, Thomas Cook, pair of candlesticks; 17th, Edward Barker, a water pot; 18th, Robert Purvis, a spittoon; 19th, Edward Pearson, a butter pot.
Journal of Horticulture, November 1877

Collect leaves and other refuse for manure, and other purposes. Prepare protection for such things as *endive*, *lettuces* and *celery*.

In the middle or towards the latter end of this month, is a proper season to plant some early *beans* ... Let these beans be planted in a warm dry situation, and some in a south border, under a wall or other fence ...

Sow the Early Frame and Early Charlton *pease* on a south border, or other warm sheltered situation. These two, if sown at the same time, will form a succession. Set traps for mice, or adopt any other available means to prevent their attacking the pease.

Harry Yes, sow peas now, because you don't want them higher than 3 inches before January as it's the stems which are susceptible to frost. Coal or coke ash was often placed around the stems. It kept them free from waterlogging and also helped to ward off slugs. We used to sow mid to late November and generally used cloches.

Now also go over the *fig* trees and pull off all those autumnal green fruit which are upon the branches, for they are useless; and if left on, would injure the eyes of the young tender branches which are for next year's bearers ...
It will likewise, in time of a very hard frost, be proper to shelter some of the best fig trees by an occasional covering of mats, to protect the young shoots which are to bear next year; for they being soft and succulent, are more liable than those of other fruit trees to suffer by severe frost.

Harry I'd tidy up fig trees under glass to look workmanlike, but generally on outside figs the green fruits just drop off. I'd certainly cover fig trees with rush mats three feet from base up and protect them with light strawy manure. If the weather gets really bad you might lose the top, but there's a chance that you'd still have young growth at the base of the tree.

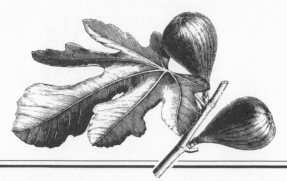

It must be confessed that digging appears at first sight, a very laborious employment, and one peculiarly unfitted to small and delicately formed hands and feet; but, by a little attention to the principles of mechanics and the laws of motion, the labour may be much simplified and rendered comparatively easy.

•

Every lady should be careful, when she has finished digging, to have her spade dipped in water, and then wiped dry; after which it should be hung up in some warm dry shed, or harness room to keep it free from rust as nothing lessens the labour of digging more than having a perfectly smooth and polished spade.

Gardening for Ladies, 1841

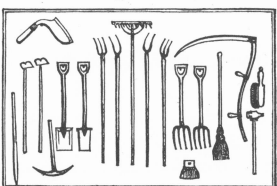

Prune *plum*, *apple*, and *pear* trees on walls and espaliers. This operation
may be performed on these trees any time this month. *Cherry* trees
on walls and espaliers may also be pruned any time this month.

Now you may transplant for the walls, where wanted, *peach*, *nectarine*,
and *apricot* trees; also *plums* and *cherries*, &c.; allotting the three
former principally the best south walls; and let some of the two latter
have also a south aspect; and you may likewise plant some of all the
sorts in west and east exposures.
The trees should be planted at the distance of at least fifteen or
eighteen feet from one another, with the stem of each tree about
three inches from the wall, and inclining thereto with the head.

Dried old *onions*, housed for winter, should be occasionally turned
over, and pick out all that discover any tendency to a decayed state.

Harry It was always a regular routine, going through all your stored fruit
and roots, and it was generally done on a wet day.

Sow the different sorts of *small salading*, where still in request, at this
season; in which, if required in constant succession, should sow some
once a week or fortnight.

Harry Sow mustard and cress under glass.

Take advantage of a dry day to tie up some *endive* plants to
whiten them.

Harry Endive needs frost protection in November. I'd prefer to have
endive inside a glasshouse by now, or put a pot over them.

Towards the end of the month, or before frost sets in, cut off the
long leaves of *artichokes* to within a foot of the ground. Dig the
latter, but so as not to cut the roots. Mulch with litter, fern, or leaves,
to protect from frost, packing the protecting material close to the
plants all round, but not over their hearts.

Harry This is, of course, the globe artichoke. If you thatch with straw or
leaves and put string around to stop the wind lifting it, when you take it
all off in spring you'll find they're as dry as anything.

Notes

A TRANSATLANTIC OBSERVER remarks that the value of bones imported annually into Britain to be used in fertilising the land are computed to be worth ten million dollars. They are obtained from Russia, Germany, South America, and the United States. Throughout Great Britain bones are collected from every possible source of supply – so valuable are bones considered in Germany that a proverb there reads: 'One ton of bone dust saves the importation of ten tons of German corn.'

Journal of Horticulture, 1877

When nuts are but few, they small and hollow,
A cold and wet harvest, there's no doubt, will follow;
But when they are plenty, and good, 'tis agreed,
A rich, golden harvest is sure to succeed.

DECEMBER

December gives unmistakable signs of winter; the last lingering leaf has fallen from the beech and oak, and it will occasion no surprise if one rise some morning to find an unvaried expanse of snow overspreading the earth.

The Book of Garden Management, 1862

Harry I always liked December. It was often very hard work for ten days getting everything ready for Christmas, but it was like going to a show. Everyone put great effort into it and the garden was cleaned up everywhere, especially the grounds. It was really all bustle. The first bulbs had to be in flower for Christmas. There would be freesias, lily of the valley, very often arum lilies and masses of chrysanthemums.

Collect all decaying substances in heaps for manure, and these may be turned when the ground, either from frost or wet, is not in a condition to be worked.

In wet weather diligently forward all work that can be done indoors, so that it may not be to do when the weather is fine. Pea sticks cut before the sap rises are stronger, and not so apt to rot, as those cut after it begins to move. They should therefore be brought in and prepared, sorting them into lengths to suit the respective heights to which the different kinds of pease grow. Then tie them up in bundles that can conveniently be carried, and place them under cover, but where air may freely circulate, till they are required for use.

In bad weather tallies should be prepared for painting, to be afterwards written with the names of seeds sown, or crops planted.

Jerusalem Artichokes – May be taken up as required fresh out of the ground; but, in case of frost, the latter should be covered over with litter.

Harry It was always good policy to cover any Jerusalem artichokes left in the ground with litter, because if you had call for them you could dig them even when the ground was frosty. A few dug and stored were always handy if the frosts became really bad.

NOTES

A Wash to Prevent the Hair from Falling Off

A quarter of an ounce of unprepared tobacco leaves, two ounces of rosemary, two ounces of box leaves, boiled in a quart of water in an earthen pipkin with a lid, for twenty minutes; strain and use this wash cold, by applying it to the roots of the hair with a hair-brush occasionally.

Housekeeper's & Butler's Assistant, 1862

DAMP FEET – HINTS TO LADIES

For the benefit of my sister gardeners, I desire to draw their attention to a very elegant *sabot*, or wooden shoe (fig. 238), by the use of which I have been enabled to paddle about in my garden with *some* degree of comfort, even during the late wet weather. I bought them of Messrs Dick Radclyffe & Co., of Holborn, at whose shop I have purchased so *many* things for use in my garden. I wear them over my slippers. But on cold days, I draw an easy *woollen* sock over my slippers before putting on the sabot; and you have no idea of the *comfort* I experience in my gardening work. These wooden sabots are a *great deal* lighter to wear than a heavy boot or golosh, and can be put on and off with *far* less trouble. The lappet, tied over the instep, holds the sabot firmly.

Mary C., Fulham   *The Villa Gardener, December 1870*

In case of frost, a portion of the best *parsley* should have a frame, or other protection placed over it.

Guard against the attacks of *mice*. These may be caught in traps; when they are, give them, at intervals, to a cat on the spot.

The fruit-room should be kept closed at night, and also during the warmest period of any day that happens to be so much warmer than usual as to cause condensation. Remove all decaying fruit; but, in so doing, disturb as little as possible that which is sound.

Mushrooms – Now take good care of the mushroom-beds, to defend them effectually from frost and wet, by continuing a good covering of clean, dry straw constantly over the beds, not less than a foot in thickness; and generally over the straw covering spread some large garden mats, which will throw the falling wet off more quickly and effectually as well as prove a greater security against frost or very cold weather.

Early Kidney-Beans in the Hothouse – Sometime in this month you may plant some early dwarf kidney-beans in pots or in boxes, and place them in the hothouse, upon the top of the bark-bed wall or front flues, &c.; by which means you will have a chance of a small early produce; as they seldom yield considerably from this season of planting.

Take care now of new-planted *fruit trees* . . . let their roots be well secured from frost . . . this must be done by laying mulch, or some kind of dungy litter, on the surface of the ground about the trees; and let this be laid full as far, each way, as you think the roots extend. Support all new-planted standard fruit trees, where wanting, with stakes; especially those with high stems and tolerably full heads, and that are in exposed situations, open to the power of winds.
In doing this, observe, previously to tying them to the stakes, to twist a piece of hay-band, or something similar, round the stem of each tree, in the part that is to be fastened to the stake, to prevent the bark from being galled or injured when the tree is rocked by the winds.

Harry It's important to stake trees, because rocked by the wind they develop a ring collar around the stump, which becomes waterlogged.

*N*OTES

THE PINE worthily holds the highest position amongst
exotic fruit ...
The fruit is most valued here at Christmas, and from our small
stock of fruiting plants I always manage to obtain a few fruits
at that time. I cut last winter about a dozen Smooth-leaved
Cayenne and Charlotte Rothschild.
Journal of Horticulture, 1871

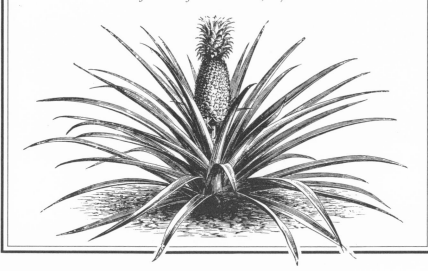

Bunches of *flowers* are at command from cold pits from October to
April inclusive. Very welcome are bunches of violets but some like
to see the flowers upon the plants, and the plants grown in pots.
What more acceptable than a stand having a panful of Lily of the
Valley in the centre, and the blue sweet violets surrounding?

Harry For a spectacular display of flowers around this time of year you can
make a cone of lily of the valley. You need a wire cone shape, some
sphagnum moss or a decent piece of moss from woodlands, and some good
forcing crowns of lily of the valley from a supplier. Pack the moss tightly
into the wire cone, then using a little dibber puncture holes in the moss
and push the crowns in. Tease the moss back over the holes. Go over the
whole cone, leaving a couple of inches between each crown to give the
leaves a chance to develop. When all the crowns are inserted, give the cone
a good watering with a fine-rosed can. Place a piece of newspaper around
the cone and put it in a warm place, around 60 to 65°F. After a few days,
growth will start and you can take the newspaper off, but still keep the heat
the same. In a week or so's time, hopefully, you'll have a nice cone of lily
of the valley for Christmas.

To Preserve a Branch or Flower in the Exact Position it Grew
Procure an earthen jar large enough to hold it without its touching
the sides, put it to stand upright in it, and carefully dribble in some
perfectly dry sand until the whole is covered. Great care should be
taken not to put out of place any of the petals or leaves, by putting
too much sand in at a time. When the whole is filled the jar must be
put to stand in a gentle oven for a few hours, when it may be taken
out and kept in any dry place till wanted. It will keep any length of
time if not taken out till wanted.

The Gardener's Receipt Book, 1861

A SELECTION OF
USEFUL SUPPLIERS

Old varieties of fruit trees

RHS Enterprises Ltd, Plant Centre, RHS Garden, Wisley, Woking,
Surrey GU23 6QB.
☎ Guildford (0483) 224234

Scotts Nurseries (Merriott) Ltd, Merriott, Somerset.
☎ Crewkerne (0460) 72306

St Bridget's Nurseries Ltd, Main Garden Centre, Old Rydon Lane, Exeter.
☎ Topsham (039 287) 3672

J.C. Allgrove Ltd, The Nurseries, Middle Green, Langley, Bucks.
☎ Slough (0753) 20155

Everton Nurseries Ltd, Everton, Nr Lymington, Hampshire SO41 0JZ.
☎ Lymington (0590) 42155

Highfield Nurseries, Whitminster, Gloucester.
☎ Gloucester (0452) 740266

Chris Bowers, Whispering Trees Nursery, Wimbotsham, Norfolk PE34 8QB.
☎ Downham Market (0366) 388752

Philip House, Family Trees, Curdridge, Botley, Southampton.
☎ Botley (04892) 6680

•

Old varieties of soft fruits

Ken Muir, Honeypot Farm, Weeley Heath, Clacton-on-Sea, Essex CO16 9BJ.
☎ Clacton (0255) 830181

Chris Bowers, Whispering Trees Nursery, Wimbotsham, Norfolk PE34 8QB.
☎ Downham Market (0366) 388752

J. Tweedie, Denby Dale Road West, Calder Grove, Wakefield, Yorks.
☎ Wakefield (0924) 274630

•

Old varieties of vegetables

Chiltern Seeds, Bortree Stile, Ulverston, Cumbria LA12 7PB.
☎ Ulverston (0229) 56946

HDRA Sales Ltd, National Centre for Organic Gardening,
Ryton-on-Dunsmore, Coventry CV8 3LG.
☎ Coventry (0203) 303517

J.W. Boyce, 67 Station Road, Soham, Ely, Cambridgeshire CB7 5ED.
☎ Ely (0353) 721819

Sutton's Seeds Ltd, Hele Road, Torquay, Devon TQ2 7QJ.
☎ Torquay (0803) 62011

•

Herbs

Suffolk Herbs, Sawyers Farm, Little Cornard, Sudbury, Suffolk CO10 0NY.
☎ Bures (0787) 227247

Hollington Nurseries, Woolton Hill, Newbury, Berks. RG15 9XT.
☎ Highclere (0635) 253908

•

Victorian violets

Groves Nurseries, Bridport, Dorset.
☎ Bridport (0308) 22654

•

Asparagus

Trevor Sore, Stock Corner Farm, Stock Corner, Beck Row,
Bury St Edmunds, Suffolk.
☎ Burnt Fen (035375) 377

•

Box hedging

Buckingham Nurseries, 3 Tingewick Road, Buckingham MK18 4AE.
☎ Buckingham (0280) 813556

•

Rhubarb and seakale forcing pots

A. Harris & Sons, Farnham Potteries, Pottery Lane, Wrecclesham,
Farnham, Surrey GU10 4QJ.
☎ Farnham (0252) 715318

•

Fertilisers and other garden requisites

Joseph Bentley Ltd, Beck Lane, Barrow-on-Humber,
South Humberside DN19 7AQ.
☎ Barrow-on-Humber (0469) 30501

•

Hurdles and straw for making straw mats

The Thatching Advisory Service, Rose Tree Farm, 29 Nine Mile Road,
Finchampstead, Wokingham, Berks. RG11 4QD.
☎ Wokingham (0734) 734203

•